# HOW TO PLAY *BETTER* GUITAR

4⁹⁵
8E

*by the author of*
HOW TO PLAY THE GUITAR

# HOW TO PLAY
# *BETTER* GUITAR

## *Jerry Silverman*

1972
Doubleday and Company, Inc.
Garden City, New York

ISBN: 0-385-00579-2
LIBRARY OF CONGRESS CATALOG CARD NUMBER 79-180109

# A WORD FROM THE AUTHOR

This book has been created as a companion volume to *How to Play the Guitar*. Any student who has become familiar with the material contained in that earlier work should be able to improve his playing considerably through *How to Play Better Guitar*.

Other guitarists, beyond their second year of study, should find plenty of interesting and challenging material contained herein.

Emphasis has necessarily been placed upon the exposition of concepts and techniques through note reading. In the past many folk guitarists, particularly those who were self-taught, shunned the more formal approach in favor of an entirely aural and imitative method of learning. While there is still much to be said for "playing by ear," it is obviously impossible to discuss complex rhythms, runs, and harmonic formulations without at least some basic understanding of musical terminology and note reading.

Accordingly, I have included here a section on Note Reading—reprinted from *How to Play the Guitar*—as an important reference and aid for those of you who may still need to brush up on that aspect of the guitar.

# CONTENTS

SECTION THREE: FOLK SONGS À LA MODE—MODAL AND PENTATONIC MELODIES

SECTION FOUR: BARRE CHORDS

## SECTION FIVE: BLUES

## SECTION SIX: FOREIGN AND FAR OUT

## SECTION SEVEN: NOTE READING

SECTION EIGHT: THE THEORY OF CHORD CONSTRUCTION

SECTION NINE: VITAL INFORMATION

SECTION ONE

# Bass Runs in Minor Keys

A bass run is a series of notes, played on the lower strings, coming at the point where one chord changes to another. Generally, but not always, the notes that make up the run are the notes of the scale that connect the roots of the two chords involved. The root of a chord is that note which gives the chord its letter name.

In $\frac{2}{4}$ or $\frac{4}{4}$ time the run begins two beats before the new chord is to be played. The run takes the place of the last two beats of the preceding chord and produces a smooth transition between the chords.

In $\frac{3}{4}$ time the run usually begins three beats—a full measure—before the new chord arrives. In that case it completely supplants the preceding chord.

Special cases involving different rhythmic solutions to the problem of "fitting in" runs will be dealt with in the music itself as they arise.

The subject of bass runs in *major* keys—pertaining to the fundamental chords—has been gone into extensively in the beginning volume in this series, *How to Play the Guitar*. There it was possible to select a representative number of songs in the five basic major guitar keys (C, G, D, A and E) and illustrate how runs involving the I, IV, V, and occasionally the II chords are played.

In minor keys, however, such regularity is not possible. Chord progressions are generally more varied and less predictable than in correspondingly "simple" folk songs in major keys. Therefore, I have not tried to formulate a "table of bass runs in minor keys," but have rather treated each of the following songs as more or less unique in terms of its chord and run content.

The keys to be covered are the three common minor keys that guitarists favor: *A minor, D minor,* and *E minor.* In cases where the range may be too high or too low for you to sing comfortably a judicious use of the capo is advised.

At this point—and throughout this book—the ability to read music would be of great help. Those of you who cannot already do so would be well advised to spend some time with Section Seven, acquainting yourselves with the fundamentals of note reading.

To make things easier, though, I will give string and fret numbers in this section for the notes of the runs. The first number is the string and the second number is the fret. For example: 5/0 = fifth string, open; 6/3 = sixth string, third fret.

## Peter Gray

14

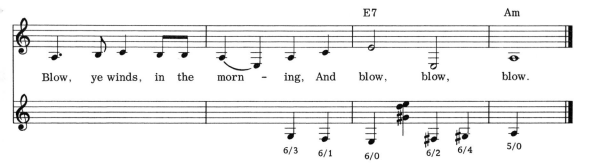

Blow, ye winds, in the morn - ing, And blow, blow, blow.

6/3  6/1  6/0  6/2  6/4  5/0

Am
Now, Peter fell in love all with

E7
A nice young girl.

The first two letters of her name

    E7       Am
Were Luc-i-anna Quirl. *Chorus*


Am
Just as they were a-going to wed

  E7       Am
Her father did say no;

And quin-ci-contly she was sent

E7      Am
Beyond the O-hi-o. *Chorus*


        Am
When Peter heard his love was lost,

  E7       Am
He knew not what to say;

He'd half a mind to jump into

E7      Am
The Susquehan-i-ay. *Chorus*

Am
But he went traveling to the west

  E7       Am
For furs and other skins;

Till he was caught and scal-pi-ed

  E7      Am
By blood-i In-ji-ins. *Chorus*


      Am
When Luc-i-anna heard the news

    E7      Am
She straightway took to bed,

And never did get up again

  E7     Am
Until she di-i-ed. *Chorus*


      Am
You fathers all a warning take—

  E7      Am
Each one as has a girl;

And think upon poor Peter Gray

  E7      Am
And Luc-i-anna Quirl. *Chorus*

# Drill, Ye Tarriers, Drill

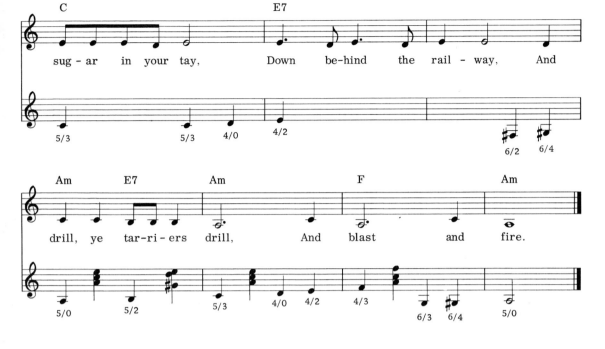

sug - ar in your tay, Down be-hind the rail - way, And drill, ye tar-ri-ers drill, And blast and fire.

Am
Our new foreman was Jim McCann,

E7
By God, he was a blame mean man;

Am
Last week a premature blast went off,

E7
And a mile in the air went Big Jim Goff. *Chorus*

Am
The next time pay day come around,

E7
Jim Goff a dollar short was found.

Am
When he asked what for come this reply,

E7
"Yer docked fer the time you wuz up in the sky!" *Chorus*

Am
Our boss was a fine man down to the ground,

E7
And he married a lady six foot 'round.

Am
She baked good bread and she baked it well,

E7
But she baked it hard as the holes in hell. *Chorus*

17

# Wayfaring Stranger

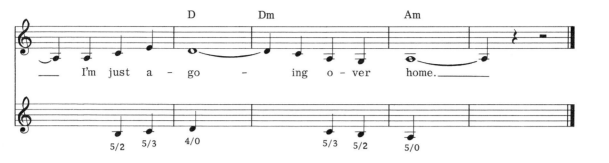

I'm just a - go - ing o - ver home.

5/2  5/3  4/0     5/3  5/2  5/0

# Moscow Nights

Original Russian lyrics by M. Matusovskii. Music by V. Solovyov-Sedoi.

Still-ness in the grove not a rust - ling sound,
*Nye slysh-ny v sa - du da - zhe sho - ro - khi,*

Guitar
5/2  5/3  4/0  4/0  4/1  4/2  6/2  6/4  5/0  5/0  5/2

Soft - ly shines the moon clear and bright. Dear, if
*Vsyo zdyes za - mer - lo do oo - tra. Yes - li b*

5/3  4/0  4/2  4/3  6/3  5/0  5/2  5/3  4/2  4/1  4/0

you could know___ how___ I trea-sure so___ This most
*zna - li vy,___ kak___ mnye do - ro - gi___ Pod - mos -*

5/3  5/2  5/4  4/0  4/2  4/0

19

beau - ti - ful Mos - cow night.
*kov - ni - ye ve - che - ra.*

night.
*ra.*

5/3  5/2  5/0  6/0  6/2  6/4  5/0

Am          Dm          E7       Am
Lazily the brook, like a silv'ry stream

C              F  G7        C
Ripples gently in the moonlight;

B7  E7  Am                    Dm
And  a  song afar fades as in a dream

        Am          E7        Am
In the spell of this summer night.


Am              Dm          E7        Am
Dearest, why so sad, why the downcast eyes,

C                    F   G7       C
And your lovely head bent so low?

B7  E7  Am                    Dm
Oh, it's hard to speak—and yet not to speak

        Am          E7        Am
Of the longing my heart does know.


Am              Dm          E7        Am
Promise me, my love, as the dawn appears,

C                      F   G7       C
And the darkness turns into light,

B7    E7    Am                        Dm
That you'll cherish, dear, through the passing years,

        Am          E7        Am
This most beautiful Moscow night.

```
  Am          Dm          E7    Am
Rechka dvizhetsia i nye dvizhetsia,

  C            F  G7   C
Vsia iz lunnovo serebra.

 B7  E7 Am              Dm
Pyesnia slyshitsia i nye slyshitsia

        Am     E7  Am
V eti tikhiye vechera.


  Am          Dm           E7  Am
Chto zy ty milaia  smotrish iskosa,

  C         F  G7     C
Nizko golovu naklonia?

 B7 E7 Am               Dm
Trudno vyskazat in nye vyskazat

           Am        E7      Am
Vsyo,chto na serdtse oo menia.


  Am          Dm          E7   Am
A rassvyet oozhe vsyo zametneye...

  C            F   G7     C
Tak,pozhaluista, bood dobra.

 B7 E7 Am              Dm
Nye zabood i ty eti letniye

          Am      E7  Am
Podmoskovniye vechera.
```

# The Praties, They Grow Small

Oh, the pra-ties they grow small o-ver here, o-ver

here. Oh, the pra-ties they grow small o-ver here.____

Oh, the pra-ties they grow small and we dig them in the

Fall, And we eat them skin and all, o-ver here o-ver here.

Dm
Oh, I wish that we were geese,

Am     Dm   Am     Dm
Night and morn, night and morn.

Oh, I wish that we were geese,

Am     Dm
Night and morn.

Oh, I wish that we were geese,
          Gm
For they fly and take their ease,

      Dm
And they live and die in peace,

Am   Dm  Am     Dm
Eating corn, eating corn.

Dm
Oh, we're trampled in the dust,

Am  Dm  Am  Dm
Over here, over here.

Oh, we're trampled in the dust,

Am  Dm
Over here.

Oh, we're trampled in the dust,
          Gm
But the Lord in whom we trust

     Dm
Will give us crumb for crust,

Am   Dm  Am    Dm
Over here, over here.

*Repeat first verse.*

# Johnny, I Hardly Knew You

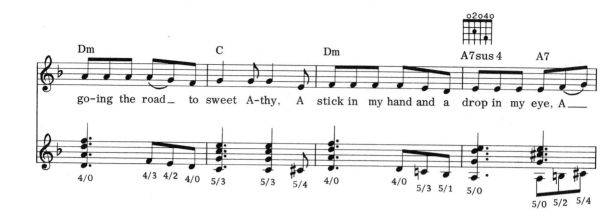

go-ing the road_ to sweet A-thy, A stick in my hand and a drop in my eye, A___

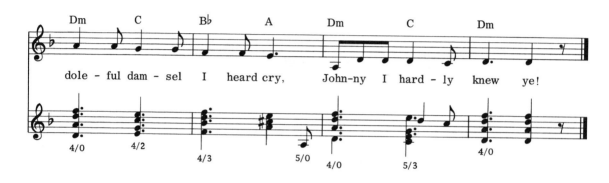

dole - ful dam - sel I heard cry, John-ny I hard - ly knew ye!

                  Dm
*Chorus:* With your drums and guns and guns and drums,

       Am
Hurroo! Hurroo!

       Dm
With your drums and guns and guns and drums,

       F
Hurroo! Hurroo!

       Dm             C
With your drums and guns and guns and drums

           A7sus4 A7
The enemy nearly slew ye,

      Dm     C    Bb      A
Oh, darling dear, ye look so queer,

       Dm     C   Dm
Faith, Johnny, I hardly knew ye!

         Dm
Where are your eyes that looked so mild,

       Am
Hurroo! Hurroo!

24

```
        Dm
Where are your eyes that looked so mild,

    F
Hurroo! Hurroo!

        Dm                      C
Where are your eyes that looked so mild
  Dm              A7sus4   A7
When my heart you   so    beguiled,
      Dm      C      Bb         A
Why did you run from me and the child?
      Dm       C    Dm
Why Johnny, I hardly knew ye!  Chorus



        Dm
Where are the legs with which you run,

    Am
Hurroo! Hurroo!

        Dm
Where are the legs with which you run,

    F
Hurroo! Hurroo!

        Dm                   C
Where are the legs with which you run
  Dm                    A7sus4   A7
When you went for to  carry a gun?
      Dm        C      Bb        A
Indeed, your dancing days are done,
        Dm       C    Dm
Faith, Johnny, I hardly knew ye!  Chorus



        Dm
I'm happy for to see you home,

    Am
Hurroo! Hurroo!

        Dm
I'm happy for to see you home,

    F
Hurroo! Hurroo!

      Dm           C
I'm happy for to see you home,

      Dm            A7sus4   A7
All from the Island  of  Ceylon,
      Dm      C      Bb       A
So low in flesh so high in bone,
        Dm       C    Dm
Faith, Johnny, I hardly knew ye!  Chorus
```

# Peat Bog Soldiers

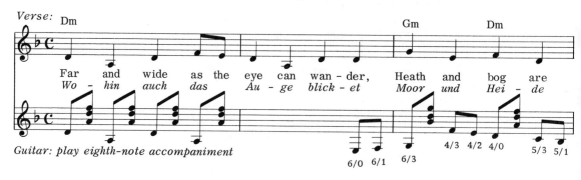

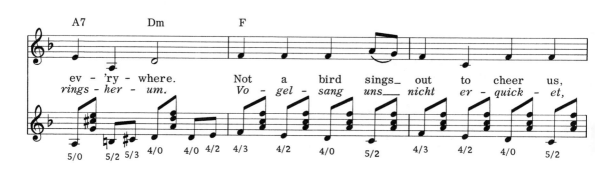

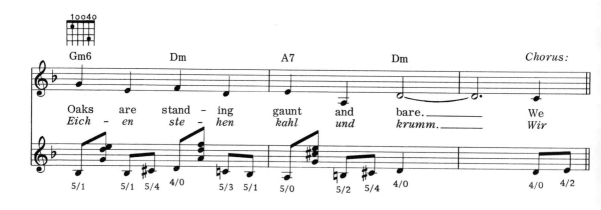

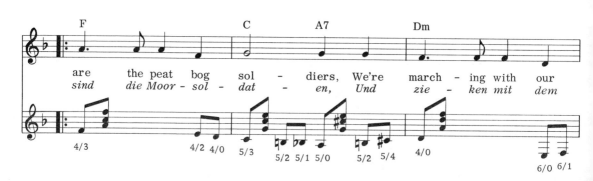

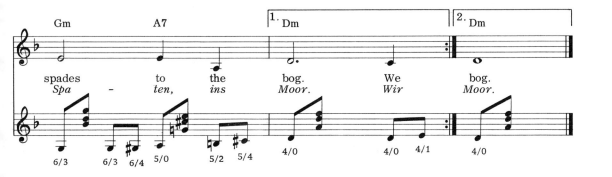

Dm
Up and down the guards are pacing,

Gm     Dm     A7     Dm
No one, no one can get through.

    F
Flight would mean a sure death facing,

Gm6     Dm     A7     Dm
Guns and barbed wire greet our view.     *Chorus*


Dm
But for us there is no complaining,

Gm     Dm     A7     Dm
Winter will in time be past.

    F
One day we shall cry rejoicing:

Gm6     Dm     A7     Dm
Homeland, dear, you're mine at last.


        F              C  A7
: Then will the peat bog soldiers

   Dm                    Gm  A7   Dm
March no more with their spades to the bog.

27

Dm  
*Auf und nieder gehen die Posten*

 Gm     Dm     A7      Dm  
*Keiner, keiner kahn hindurch.*

    F  
*Flucht wird nur das Leben kosten,*

 Gm6    Dm     A7      Dm  
*Fielfach ist umzäunt die Burg.   Chorus*


   Dm  
*Doch für uns gibt es kein Klagen,*

 Gm   Dm      A7     Dm  
*Ewig kann's nicht Winter sein.*

    F  
*Einmal werden froh wir sagen,*

 Gm6    Dm     A7      Dm  
*"Heimat, du bist wieder mein."*


*Final*          F                  C A7  
*Chorus: Dann ziehen die Moorsoldaten*

      Dm              Gm  A7    Dm  
*Nicht mehr mit dem Spaten ins Moor.*

# The Erie Canal

*Chorus:*

inch of the way From Al - ban - y to___ Buf - fa - lo.___ Low bridge,

ev - 'ry - bod - y down. Low bridge, for we're com - in' to a town. And you'll

al - ways know your neigh - bor, You'll al - ways know your pal, If you've

ev - er nav - i - gat - ed on the E - rie Ca - nal. We E - rie Ca - nal.

30

```
      Dm               Gm      A7
We better be on our way old pal,
 Dm                A7      Dm
Fifteen miles on the Erie Canal.

           Dm               Gm       A7
'Cause you bet your life I'd never part from Sal,
 Dm                A7      Dm
Fifteen miles on the Erie Canal.
       F                      C
Get up there, mule, here comes a lock,
 Dm                      A7
We'll make Rome 'bout six o'clock.

 Dm            Gm      A7
One more trip and back we'll go,
 Dm              A7    Dm - C
Right back home to Buffalo.      Chorus
```

```
 Dm            Gm      A7
Drop a tear for big–foot Sal,
   Dm                  A7      Dm
The best damn cook on the Erie Canal.

   Dm               Gm       A7
She aimed for heaven but she went to hell,
 Dm              A7      Dm
Fifteen miles on the Erie Canal.
       F                    C
The missioner said she died in sin,
   Dm                      A7
The captain said it was too much gin.

       Dm              Gm       A7
There weren't no bar where she hadn't been,
   Dm        A7    Dm - C
From Albany to Buffalo.      Chorus
```

# The Leatherwing Bat

Chorus:

Em           G
Towdy owdy dil do dum,

C    D7   G
Towdy owdy dil do day,

Em
Towdy owdy dil do dum,

B7   Em
Tol lol li dy dil do day.


Em                        G
"Hi!" said the blackbird, sitting on a chair,

C    D7     G
"Once I courted a lady fair.

Em
She proved fickle and turned her back,

B7      Em
And ever since then I've dressed black."   *Chorus*


Em                        G
"Hi!" said the little mourning dove,

C    D7     G
"I'll tell you how to regain her love.

32

```
                  Em
Court her night and court her day,

            B7      Em
Never give her time to say, 'Oh nay.'"  Chorus


    Em                            G
"Hi!" said the woodpecker, sitting on a bench,

   C      D7       G
"Once I courted a handsome wench,

                 Em
She got sulky and from me fled,

            B7        Em
And ever since then my head's been red."  Chorus


    Em                         G
"Hi!" said the blue jay as she flew,

      C          D7       G
"If I were a young man I'd have two.

                   Em
If one got saucy and wanted to go,

      B7         Em
I'd tie a new string to my bow."  Chorus
```

33

# Sometimes I Feel Like A Motherless Child

Em
Sometimes I feel like I'm almost gone.

Am                              Em
Sometimes I feel like I'm almost gone.

                    C
Sometimes I feel like I'm almost gone,

      Am        Em      B7 - Em
Way up in that heavenly land,

                    C        B7      Em
Way up in that heavenly land.

True believer!

                                      Am - Em
Way up in that heavenly land.

                              B7        Em
Way up in that heavenly land.

# All The Pretty Little Horses

Em              Am
Hush-a bye, don't you cry,

D7    B7        Em
Go to sleepy, little baby.

               Am
Way down yonder in the meadow

D7    B7        Em
Lies a poor little lambie.

                      G                     C
The bees and the butterflies pecking out its eyes,

            Am        B7        Em
The poor little thing cried, "Mammy."

                  Am
Hush-a bye, don't you cry,

D7    B7        Em
Go to sleepy, little baby.

# Johnny Has Gone For A Soldier

Here I sit on But-ter-milk Hill, Who could blame me, Cry my fill, And ev - 'ry tear would turn a mill, John-ny has gone for a sol - dier.

Em    Bm    Em
Me oh my, I loved him so,

   G                              Em
Broke my heart to see him go,

                             C
And only time will heal my woe:

             Bm       Em
Johnny has gone for a soldier.


     Em    Bm    Em
I'll sell my flax, I'll sell my wheel,

   G                              Em
Buy my love a sword of steel,

                    C
So it in battle he may wield:

             Bm       Em
Johnny has gone for a soldier.

SECTION TWO

# All Kinds of Picking

## Double-Thumbing

The term "double-thumbing" refers to a style of playing wherein the right thumb and one or more of the fingers alternate in the playing of chordal, rhythmic, and melodic passages.

A very effective double-thumbing pattern utilizes a thumb-chord brush stroke as well as the thumb-finger alternation.

Finger a C chord.

Strike the bass note (C) with your thumb and follow with a loose-wrist downstroke with the nails over the rest of the chord.

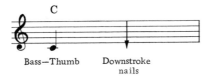

You should have no difficulty keeping up a steady one-two—one-two beat. Thumb-nails—thumb-nails . . .

Now, maintaining the C chord with your left hand play the following figure: Thumb plays fourth string (now E), first finger plays second string (now C), thumb plays third string (G), first finger plays second string again.

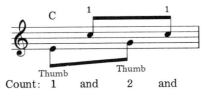

When you put the brush stroke and the double-thumbing together to form the complete pattern, pay close attention to the timing. The brush stroke is made up of two quarter notes ("one-two"), and the double-thumbing is made up of four eighth notes ("three-and-four-and").

Count:  1    2    3  and  4  and    1    2    3  and  4  and

Try a similar pattern with an F chord. Observe the different strings involved.

Double-thumbing may be used to play melodies as well as accompaniments. For the playing of melody you have to be prepared to move certain fingers of the left hand from time to time. You can't be frozen to the chord forever. Melody demands movement. Each song is different. You never know what you're going to encounter until you actually begin to play.

Sing *John Hardy* using your brand new double-thumbing pattern. Then play the guitar solo written out under the melody line.

## John Hardy

John Har - dy    was    a    des-p'rate lit - tle    man,    He

38

wore two guns ev - 'ry day. _____ He shot down a man on the West Vir - gin - ia line; You ought to seen John Har - dy get - tin' a - way, poor__ boy, You ought to seen John__ Har - dy get - tin' a - way. _____

John Hardy stood at the gambling table,
F                 C

Didn't have no interest in the game.
F             C

Up stepped a yellow gal and threw a dollar down,
F           C

Said, "John Hardy's playing in my name, poor boy,

John Hardy's playing in my name."

39

```
          F              C
John Hardy took that yellow gal's money,
     F              C
And then he began to play.
          F              C
Said, "The man that wins my yellow gal's dollar,

I'll lay him in his lonesome grave, poor boy,

I'll lay him in his lonesome grave."


          F              C
John Hardy drew to a four-card straight,
          F                    C
And the cowboy drew to a pair.
      F              C
John failed to catch and the cowboy won,

And he left him sitting dead in his chair, poor boy,

He left him sitting dead in his chair.


          F              C
John started to catch that east-bound train,
     F              C
So dark he could not see.
          F              C
Up stepped the police and took him by the arm,

Said, "Johnny, come and go with me, poor boy,

Johnny, come and go with me."


          F              C
John Hardy's father came to see him,
   F                  C
Come for to go his bail.
      F                    C
No bail was allowed for a murdering man,

So they shoved John Hardy back in jail, poor boy,

They shoved John Hardy back in jail.
```

    F        C
They took John Hardy to the hanging ground,

   F      C
And hung him there to die,

    F       C
And the very last words I heard him say

Were, "My forty-four never told a lie, poor boy,

My forty-four never told a lie."


    F       C
"I've been to the east and I've been to the west,

   F        C
I've travelled this whole world around.

   F       C
I've been to the river and I've been baptized,

And now I'm on my hanging ground, poor boy,

Now I'm on my hanging ground."


Just as the thumb alternates from string to string, so may the "answer-back" notes. When this higher (treble) string alternation is desired, it is better to use more than one finger.

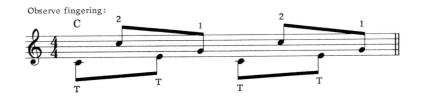

You don't have to become locked into any particular right-hand pattern. It is always effective to vary the proceedings. Be on the lookout in *The Eddystone Light* and, in fact, throughout this book for changes of pace and pattern.

# The Eddystone Light

*Verse:*

My fa-ther was the keep-er of the Ed-dy-stone Light, And he slept with a mer-maid one fine night. From this un-ion there came three. Two lit-tle fish-es and the oth-er was me.

*Chorus:*

Yo ho ho, the wind blows free. Oh, for the life on the roll-ing sea.

C
One night as I was a-trimming of the glim,

   F   G7    C
And a-singing a verse from the evening hymn,

A voice from the starboard shouted, "Ahoy!"

   F   G7  C
And there was my mother a-sitting on a bouy. *Chorus*

42

C
"Oh, what has become of my children three?"

F    G7     C
My mother then she said to me.

"One was exhibited as a talking fish,

     F         G7      C
And the other was served on a chafing dish." *Chorus*


            C
Then the phosphorous flashed in her seaweed hair,

   F    G7       C
I looked again and my mother wasn't there.

But a voice came echoing out through the night.

    F      G7        C
"To hell with the keeper of the Eddystone Light!" *Chorus*

Another slight but effective change involves the second beat of the brush stroke. Whereas before you just brushed down with your nails, now brush the index finger up quickly after the downstroke. Two eighths instead of one quarter.

And of course that can be combined with the double-thumbing.

# Miners' Lifeguard

Watch the ___ and your eye_____ up - on the scale._____

**Chorus:** Un - ion min - ers stand to - geth - er,_____ Heed no op - er - a - tor's tale._____

___ Keep your hands_____ up - on the dol - lar_____ And your eyes_____ up - on the scale._____

*Continue for other verses*

45

                G  
You've been docked and docked, my boys,

           C               G  
You've been loading two to one.

What have you to show for working

            A7           D - D7  
Since this labor had begun?

      G  
Overalls and cans for rockers,

           C              G  
In your shanties sleep on rails:

Keep your hand upon the dollar,

               D7         G  
And your eye     upon the scale.  *Chorus*


           G  
In conclusion bear in memory,

           C               G  
Keep this watchword in your mind,

"God provides for every nation

           A7           D - D7  
When in union they combine."

            G  
Stand like men and link together,

        C             G  
Victory for you'll prevail:

Keep your hand upon the dollar,

               D7         G  
And your eye     upon the scale.  *Chorus*

The thumb may also play certain selected nonchordal notes as part of its alternating pattern.

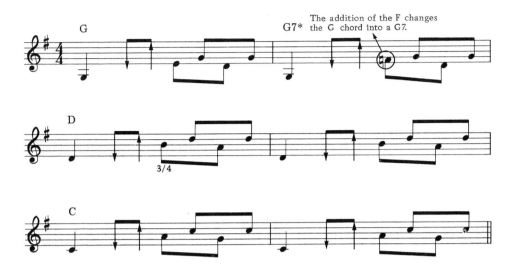

## Mama Don't Allow

Ma-ma don't 'low no gui - tar pick-in' 'round here._____

Ma-ma don't 'low no gui - tar pick-in' 'round here._____

I don't care what ma-ma don't 'low, Gon-na pick my gui - tar an - y - how,

Ma-ma don't 'low no gui - tar pick-in' 'round here._____

G
Mama don't 'low no banjo playin' 'round here.

                                               D
Mama don't 'low no banjo playin' 'round here.

G                 G7
I  don't care what mama don't 'low,

           C
Gonna play my banjo anyhow.

 G                 D                   G
Mama don't 'low no banjo playin' 'round here.


        G                                            G
Mama don't 'low no cigar smokin' 'round here.

                                                D
Mama don't 'low no cigar smokin' 'round here.

G                 G7
I  don't care what mama don't 'low,

           C
Gonna smoke my cigar anyhow.

 G                 D                   G
Mama don't 'low no cigar smokin' 'round here.


        G
Mama don't 'low no honky-tonkin' 'round here.

                                               D
Mama don't 'low no honky-tonkin' 'round here.

G                G7
I  don't care what mama don't 'low,

           C
Gonna honky-tonk some anyhow,

 G                 D                   G
Mama don't 'low no honky-tonkin' 'round here.


        G
Mama don't 'low no midnight ramblin' 'round here.

                                                D
Mama don't 'low no midnight ramblin' 'round here.

G
I  don't care what mama don't 'low,

           C
Gonna ramble midnights anyhow.

 G                 D                   G
Mama don't 'low no midnight ramblin' 'round here.

## Going Down the Road

I'm go - ing down the road feel - ing bad, Oh Lord, I'm go - ing down the road feel - ing bad. I'm

continue

go - ing down the road feel - ing bad, Lord, Lord,— And I ain't gon - na be treat - ed this - a way._____

D
Two-dollar shoes hurt my feet, oh Lord,

G               D
Two-dollar shoes hurt my feet.

G               D
Two-dollar shoes hurt my feet, Lord, Lord,

      A7             D
And I ain't gonna be treated this-a way.


D
Ten-dollar shoes fit me fine, oh Lord,

G               D
Ten-dollar shoes fit me fine.

G               D
Ten-dollar shoes fit me fine, Lord, Lord,

      A7             D
And I ain't gonna be treated this-a way.


D
I'm here in the jailhouse on my knees, oh Lord,

   G               D
I'm here in the jailhouse on my knees.

   G               D
I'm here in the jailhouse on my knees, Lord, Lord,

      A7             D
And I ain't gonna be treated this-a way.

  D
They fed me on corn bread and peas, oh Lord,
  G          D
They fed me on corn bread and peas.
  G          D
They fed me on corn bread and peas, Lord, Lord,
  A7          D
And I ain't gonna be treated this-a way.


  D
I'm goin' where the climate suits my clothes, oh Lord,
  G          D
I'm goin' where the climate suits my clothes.
  G          D
I'm goin' where the climate suits my clothes, Lord, Lord,
  A7          D
And I ain't gonna be treated this-a way.


  D
I'm goin' where the water tastes like wine, oh Lord,
  G          D
I'm goin' where the water tastes like wine.
  G          D
I'm goin' where the water tastes like wine, Lord, Lord,
    A7            D
'Cause the water 'round here tastes like turpentine.

*Repeat Verse One.*

Alternating upper and lower notes.

# John Henry

Well,_ ev - 'ry Mon - day_ morn - ing,

*Guitar solo*

When the blue-birds be - gin to sing,

You can see John Hen - ry_

out on the line, You can hear John

Hen-ry's ham - mer ring, Lord, Lord,_ You can hear John

Hen-ry's ham-mer ring. You can ring.

D
When John Henry was a little baby,

            D7      A7
A-sitting on his papa's knee,

      D                 G7
He picked up a hammer and a little piece of steel,

     D
Said, "Hammer's gonna be the death of me, Lord, Lord,

Hammer's gonna be the death of me."

       D
Well, the captain said to John Henry,

           D7      A7
"Gonna bring me a steam drill 'round,

      D            G7
Gonna bring me a steam drill out on the job,

      D
Gonna whup that steel on down, Lord, Lord,

Gonna whup that steel on down."

     D
John Henry said to his captain,

        D7      A7
"A man ain't nothin' but a man,

      D        G7
And before I let that steam drill beat me down,

    D
I'll die with a hammer in my hand, Lord, Lord,

I'll die with a hammer in my hand."

     D
John Henry said to his shaker,

        D7     A7
"Shaker, why don't you sing?

     D                                  G7
I'm a-throwin' twelve pounds from my hips on down,

     D
Just listen to the cold steel ring, Lord, Lord,

Listen to the cold steel ring."


     D
John Henry said to his shaker,

        D7     A7
"Shaker, why don't you pray?

     D       G7
'Cause if I miss this little piece of steel,

     D
Tomorrow be your buryin' day, Lord, Lord,

Tomorrow be your buryin' day."


     D
John Henry was driving on the mountain,

        D7     A7
And his hammer was flashing fire.

     D                G7
And the last words I heard that poor boy say,

        D
"Gimme a cool drink of water 'fore I die, Lord, Lord,

Gimme a cool drink of water 'fore I die."


     D
John Henry, he drove fifteen feet,

        D7     A7
The steam drill only made nine.

     D                  G7
But he hammered so hard that he broke his poor heart,

     D
And he laid down his hammer and he died, Lord, Lord,

He laid down his hammer and he died.

        D
They took John Henry to the graveyard

              D7      A7
And they buried him  in  the  sand.

     D                               G7
And every locomotive comes a-roaring by says,

     D
"There lies a steel-driving man, Lord, Lord,

There lies a steel-driving man."


Depending on the chords involved, the thumb can play three different strings.

In *Old Dan Tucker* there are two places where a chord change occurs in the middle of a measure. In those cases the pattern is interrupted as follows:

# Old Dan Tucker

*Verse:*

Went to town the oth - er night to hear a noise and see a fight. All the peo-ple were a - run-ning a - round, Cry-ing, "Old Dan Tuck-er's come to town."

*Chorus:*

Get out the way, Old Dan Tuck - er, You're too late to come for sup - per, Sup - per's o - ver and din - ner's cook-in', And Old Dan Tuck-er just stand-in' there look - in'.

A
Old Dan Tucker's a fine old man,

E7
Washed his face in a frying pan.

A
Combed his hair with a wagon wheel

      E7  A
And died with a toothache in his heel. *Chorus*


A
Old Dan Tucker come to town,

E7
Riding a billygoat, leading a hound.

A
Hound barked and the billygoat jumped,

     E7    A
Throwed old Dan right straddle of a stump. *Chorus*

A
Old Dan Tucker clumb a tree,

           E7
His Lord and Master for to see.

     A
The limb, it broke and Dan got a fall,

           E7     A
Never got to see his Lord at all. *Chorus*


     A
Old Dan Tucker he got drunk,

            E7
Fell in the fire and he kicked up a chunk.

   A
Red-hot coal got in his shoe,

           E7     A
Lord godamighty, how the ashes flew! *Chorus*


     A
Old Dan Tucker come to town,

           E7
Swinging the ladies 'round and 'round.

   A
First to the right and then to the left,

           E7     A
And then to the one that you love best. *Chorus*


Another variation.

And a chord change on the third beat of the measure.

## Ain't It A Shame

Ain't it a shame— to beat your wife on Sun - day, ain't it a shame?____

—— Ain't it a shame— to beat your wife on Sun - day,

ain't it a shame?_____ Ain't it a shame— to beat your

wife on Sun - day, When you got Mon - day, Tues - day, We'n's-day, Oh,

Thurs - day, Fri - day, Sat - ur - day, ain't it a shame?__

    E
Ain't it a shame to kiss the girls on Sunday,

    A            E - A - E
Ain't it a shame?

Ain't it a shame to kiss the girls on Sunday,

    B7
Ain't it a shame?

    E                      E7
Ain't it a shame to kiss the girls on Sunday,

```
 A                          E
When you got Monday, Tuesday, Wednesday,

 A      E
Oh, Thursday, Friday, Saturday,

 A                  E
Ain't it a shame?


 E
Ain't it a shame to take a drink on Sunday,
 A                E  -  A  -  E
Ain't it a shame?

Ain't it a shame to take a drink on Sunday,
 B7
Ain't it a shame?
 E                      E7
Ain't it a shame to take a drink on Sunday,
 A                          E
When you got Monday, Tuesday, Wednesday,
 A      E
Oh, Thursday, Friday, Saturday,
 A                  E
Ain't it a shame?
```

## Syncopated Three-Finger Picking

Finger a C chord.
Pluck thumb (fifth string) and third finger (first string) together.
Second finger (second string)
First finger (third string)
Third finger (first string)
Thumb (fifth string)
Second finger (second string)
First finger (first string)
Follow the musical example and pay strict attention to the rhythm.

Right hand 3   2   1   3      2   1
        Thumb           Thumb

Now try the same pattern but alternate the bass from the fifth to the sixth strings for the C chord. Observe the alternation for the other chords.

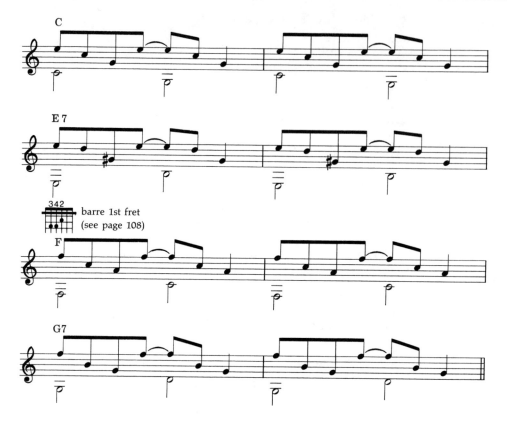

## Railroad Bill, (1)

Rail-road Bill, Rail-road Bill, He nev - er

worked and he nev - er will, I'm gon-na ride old Rail - road Bill.____

    C
Railroad Bill, he was a mighty mean man,
    E7                                            F
He shot the midnight lantern out the brakeman's hand,
              C      G7       C
I'm gonna ride old Railroad Bill.


    C
Railroad Bill took my wife,
     E7                                 F
Said, if I didn't like it he would take my life,
              C      G7       C
I'm gonna ride old Railroad Bill.


   C
Going up on the mountain, going out west,
   E7                               F
"Thirty-eight special" sticking out of my vest,
             C      G7       C
I'm gonna ride old Railroad Bill.


           C
I've got a "thirty-eight special" on a "forty-four frame,"
          E7                              F
How in the world can I miss him when I've got dead aim,
             C      G7       C
I'm gonna ride old Railroad Bill.


   C
Buy me a pistol just as long as my arm,
 E7                     F
Kill everybody ever done me harm,
             C      G7       C
I'm gonna ride old Railroad Bill.


   C
Honey, honey, think I'm a fool,
  E7                                  F
Think I would quit you when the weather is cool?
             C      G7       C
I'm gonna ride old Railroad Bill.

Since this pattern emphasizes the first string, if we can get a melody to fall conveniently on that string, we can use it to play the tune. If at some point the melody descends to the second string, the right hand has to move with it. When that happens the third finger will play the second string, and the other fingers will move down one string each as well. The thumb continues to play its customary bass notes.

## Railroad Bill, (2)

In addition to alternate basses notes may be alternated on the upper strings.

# On A Monday

63

all, al - most done. Well it's

all, Al - most done, And I

ain't gon - na see them — pret-ty girls no more.

           C                                      G -  G7  
On-a Monday me and my baby was a-walkin',

                                   C  
On-a Tuesday she locked me out of doors.

                                      G -  G7  
On-a Wednesday were settin' down a-talkin',

                                   C  
On-a Thursday she pawned all of my clothes. *Chorus*

                        C                           G -  G7  
Take these stripes, stripes from 'round my shoulder,

                                      C  
Take these chains, chains from 'round my leg.

                  C                      G    G7  
Lord, these stripes, stripes sure don't worry me,

                                   C  
But these chains, chains gonna kill me dead. *Chorus*

# The Midnight Special

Let the Mid - night Spe - cial_ shine her ev - er lov - in'

light on me._ If you ev - er go to

E7       A          E
 Now, if you ever go to Houston, Lord, you better walk right.
         B7         E7
 And you better not stagger, yes, you better not fight,
           A         E
 'Cause the sheriff will arrest you, and he'll carry you down.
          B7        E
 You can bet your bottom dollar, you're penitentiary bound. *Chorus*


E7       A          E
 Yonder comes Miss Rosie, tell me how do you know?
        B7         E7
 I know her by her apron and the dress she wore.
          A         E
 Umberella on her shoulder, piece of paper in her hand,
         B7         E
 Well, I heard her tell the captain, "Turn a-loose my man." *Chorus*


E7       A          E
 Lord, Thelma said she loved me, but I believe she told a lie,
         B7       E7
 'Cause she hasn't been to see me since last July.
          A         E
 Well, she brought me little coffee and she brought me little tea,
         B7         E
 She brought me nearly everything except the jailhouse key. *Chorus*

E7                          A                          E
   Well, the biscuits on the table, just as hard as any rock,

        B7                          E7
   If you try to eat them, break a convict's heart.

           A                          E
   My sister wrote a letter, my mother wrote a card—

             B7                          E
   "If you want to come to see us, you'll have to ride the rods."  *Chorus*


E7                          A                          E
   I'm goin' away to leave you, and my time it ain't long,

        B7                          E7
   The man is gonna call me and I'm goin' home.

           A                          E
   Then I'll be done all my grievin', whoopin' hollerin' and cryin',

           B7                          E
   Then I'll be done all my studyin' about my great long time.  *Chorus*


Here are a couple of new positions for some old familiar chords.

67

# Salty Dog

*The verses are sung to the first eight measures of the chorus.*

G                  E7
Down in the wildwood sitting on a log,

A                 A7
Singing a song about a salty dog.

D7                G - D7
Honey, let me be your salty dog.    *Chorus*


G                 E7
Two old maids a-sitting in the sand,

A                 A7
Each one wishing that the other was a man.

D7               G - D7
Honey, let me be your salty dog.    *Chorus*

68

```
  G                   E7
Worst day I ever had in my life,
            A                      A7
When my best friend caught me kissing his wife.
D7                        G - D7
Honey, let me be your salty dog.    Chorus


  G                       E7
God made a woman and He made her mighty funny,
            A                           A7
When you kiss her 'round the mouth just as sweet as any honey.
D7                         G - D7
Honey, let me be your salty dog.    Chorus
```

You can get some interesting moving bass lines. In this case the chord remains fundamentally the same, but as the notes descend different harmonic nuances are introduced.

Watch out for changes on the third beat.

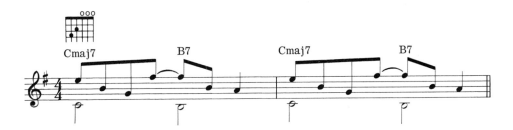

# Willie The Weeper

Did you ev-er hear the sto-ry of\_\_\_ Wil-lie the Weep-er?\_

Wil-lie the Weep-er was a chim-ney sweep-er. He had the dope hab-it and he

*Hold it!*

had it bad.\_\_\_ Lis-ten while I tell you 'bout the

dream__ he had.__ Hi dee hi dee hi,__ Ho di ho__ di ho.__

Em
He went down to the dope house one Saturday night,

Am                                              B7
When he knew that all the lights would be burning bright.

Em
He must have smoked a dozen pills or more,

    Cmaj7    Am7              B7        Em
When  he  woke up he was on a foreign shore.  *Chorus*


Em
Well, the Queen of Sheba was the first he met,

Am                                          B7
She called him her darling and her loving pet.

Em
She gave him a great big automobile,

    Cmaj7    Am7                B7            Em
With a diamond headlight and a gold steering wheel.  *Chorus*


Em
He landed with a splash in the River Nile,

Am                              B7
A-riding a domesticated crocodile.

Em
He winked at Cleopatra—she said,"Ain't he a sight'

Cmaj7        Am7            B7        Em
How  about a date for next Saturday night?"  *Chorus*

Em
Down in Monte Carlo he won every bet,

Am                              B7
Made a million dollars just a-playing roulette.

     Em
He broke the Czar of Russia—what a joke!

   Cmaj7        Am7              B7        Em
So Willie took another pill and rolled a smoke.   *Chorus*


     Em
He had a million cattle and he had a million sheep,

   Am                          B7
He had a million vessels the ocean deep.

     Em
He had a million dollars in nickels and dimes,

   Cmaj7                  Am7        B7        Em
He knew 'cause he had counted it a million times.   *Chorus*


     Em
He landed in New York one evening late,

     Am                       B7
And asked his sugar for an after date.

Em
Willie got funny, she began to shout—

     Cmaj7      Am7      B7        Em
When,   bim  bam boo! the dope gave out.   *Chorus*

72

# Joshua Fought The Battle Of Jericho

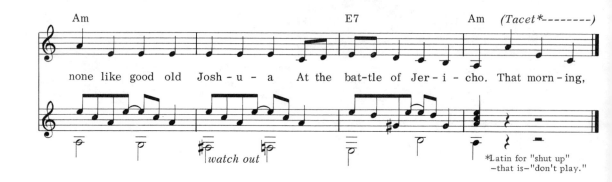

none like good old Josh-u - a  At the bat-tle of Jer - i - cho. That morn-ing,

*watch out*

*Latin for "shut up"*
*—that is—"don't play."*

Am
Up to the walls of Jericho

E7
He marched with spear in hand.

Am
"Go blow those rams horns," Joshua cried,

E7          Am
"For the battle is in my hand."

That morning. *Chorus*


Am
Then the lamb, ram, sheep horns began to blow,

E7
Trumpets began to sound.

Am
Joshua commanded the children to shout,

E7          Am
And the walls came tumbling down.

That morning. *Chorus*


Am
There's no man like Joshua,

E7
No man like Saul.

Am
No man like Joshua

E7          Am
At the battle of Jericho.

That morning. *Chorus*

74

In the following patterns a curious effect is obtained due to the fact that the note on the second string is higher in pitch than the note on the first string. The addition of the note F sharp to an *A major* chord changes the name of the chord to *A sixth*. The same F sharp in the *E seventh* chord changes the chord to *E ninth*. With the *D seventh* it is the note E that is the added factor, causing it to become *D ninth*.

Watch out for changes on the third beat.

# The Rock Island Line

Chorus:

You know the Rock Is-land Line,_ it is a might-y good road,_ You know the
Rock Is-land Line,_ it is the road to ride._ You know the
Rock Is-land Line,_ it is a might-y good road,_ And if you
want to ride it got to ride it like you're fly-in' Get your
tick-et at the sta-tion of the Rock Is-land Line._ A B C dou-ble
X Y Z, Cat's in the cup-board but he can't_ see me._

A
Moses stood on the Red Sea shore,

E7                                          A
Smiting that water with a two-by-four.  *Chorus*


A
Jesus died to save our sins,

E7                                          A
Glory to God, we're gonna need Him again.  *Chorus*


76

A
Little Evalina, sitting in the shade,

    E7                                    A
Counting all the money I ain't made.   *Chorus*


    A
If religion was a thing that money could buy,

      E7                                 A
The rich would live and the poor would die.   *Chorus*


    A
I may be right and I may be wrong,

    E7                                   A
I know you're gonna miss me when I'm gone.   *Chorus*


## Calypso Pickings

Finger an E chord.

Play a pattern of eight eighth notes as shown below, with the thumb
playing the bass on the first, fourth, and seventh notes.

It may be easier to see and feel the rhythm if the eighths are grouped
unevenly as follows:

## The Sloop John B.

*Verse:*

We come on the Sloop John B. My grand - fa - ther and me. 'Round Nas - sau Town we did roam, Drink - ing all night, We got in a fight, I feel so break-up, I want to go home.

*Chorus:*

So hoist up the John B. sails, See how the main - sail

sets. Send for the cap-tain a - shore, Let__ me go

home,_____ Let__ me go home,_____

__ Let__ me go home._____ I feel so

break-up,__ I want_ to go home._____

E
The first mate, oh, he got drunk,

Break up the people's trunk.
                                                       B7
Constable had to come and take him ashore.
                   E - E7                  A - Am
Sheriff Johnstone     please leave me alone,
             E      B7        E
I feel so break up,  I want to go home. *Chorus*

E
The poor cook, oh, he got fits,

Ate up all of the grits.
                                                 B7
Then he took and threw away all of the corn.
             E - E7                  A - Am
Sheriff Johnstone     please leave me alone,
             E      B7        E
This is the worst trip  I've ever been on. *Chorus*

In the playing of melodies sometimes adjustments and changes have to be made in the pattern.

## Choucoune

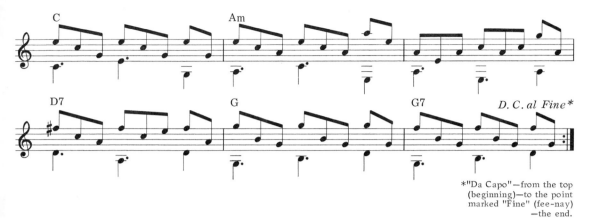

*"Da Capo"—from the top (beginning)—to the point marked "Fine" (fee-nay) —the end.

## The Six-Eight Tickle

Finger a D chord.

Play the F sharp on the first string.

Pull off the second finger (F sharp), causing the E string to sound.

Follow this by playing the note on the second string (D).

Now complete the tickle by adding the other elements.

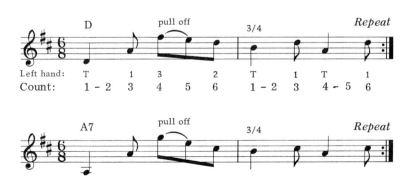

# The Farmer Is The Man

When the farm - er comes to town, With his / on - ly look and see, Then I

wa - gon bro - ken down,) / think you will a - gree,) Oh the farm - er is the man who feeds them

all.____ If you'll all.____ The farm - er is the

man,____ The farm - er is the man. Lives on cred - it 'til the

fall,____ Then they take him by the hand, And they lead him from the

land, And the mid - dle - man's the one who gets it all.____

D
When the lawyer hangs around, while the butcher cuts a pound,
A7                                              D
Oh, the farmer is the man who feeds them all.

And the preacher and the cook go a-strolling by the brook,
A7                                              D
Oh, the farmer is the man who feeds them all.

The farmer is the man, the farmer is the man,
A7
Lives on credit till the fall;

D
With the int'rest rate so high, it's a wonder he don't die,
A7                                              D
For the mortgage man's the one who gets it all.

Since the complete tickle takes two measures to play, if a chord change occurs after only one measure, we modify the pattern as follows.

## The Dodger Song

*Verse:*

Oh, the can - di - date's a dod - ger, Yes a well - known dod - ger. Oh, the can - di-date's a dod - ger, Yes and I'm a dod - ger, too.___ He'll meet you and greet you and ask you for your vote, But look out boys he's a - dod - gin' for a note.

*Chorus:*

Yes we're all___ a - dod-gin',___ a dodge, dodge, dod - gin', Yes we're all___ a - dod - gin' out our way through the world.

```
         D                              A7           D
Oh, the lawyer, he's a dodger, yes, a well-known dodger,
                                   A7           D
Oh, the lawyer, he's a dodger, yes, and I'm a dodger, too.

He'll plead your case and claim you for a friend,
  A7                              D
But look out boys, he's easy for to bend.   Chorus


         D                              A7           D
Oh, the merchant, he's a dodger, yes, a well-known dodger,
                                   A7           D
Oh, the merchant, he's a dodger, yes, and I'm a dodger, too.

He'll sell you goods at double the price,
  A7                                      D
And when you go to pay him, you'll have to pay him twice.   Chorus


         D                              A7           D
Oh, the farmer, he's a dodger, yes, a well-known dodger,
                                   A7           D
Oh, the farmer, he's a dodger, yes, and I'm a dodger, too.

He'll plow his cotton and he'll hoe his corn,
  A7                                      D
But he'll make a living just as sure as you're born.   Chorus


         D                              A7           D
Oh, the lover, he's a dodger, yes, a well-known dodger,
                                   A7           D
Oh, the lover, he's a dodger, yes, and I'm a dodger, too.

He'll hug you and kiss you and call you his bride,
  A7                              D
But look out, girls, he's a-telling you a lie.   Chorus
```

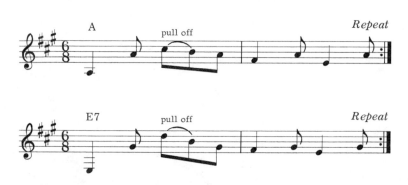

Watch out for quick changes.

# Eating Goober Peas

A Civil War song about peanuts.

*Verse:*

Sit - tin' by the road - side on a sum - mer's day,

Chat - tin' with my mess - mates, pass - in' time a - way.

Ly - in' in the shad - ows un - der-neath the trees,

Good - ness how de - li - cious, _____ eat - in' goob - er peas.

*Chorus:*

Peas, peas, peas, peas, eat - in' goob - er peas.

Good - ness how de - li - cious, _____ eat - in' goob - er peas.

85

<pre>
     A                      D              A
When a horseman passes the soldiers have a rule,
                          (Bm)        E7
To cry out at their loudest,"Mister, get a mule."
     A                      D
But still another pleasure, enchantinger than these,
     A          D     E7          A
Is wearing out your molars, eating goober peas.  Chorus


     A                      D              A
Just before the battle the gen'ral hears a row,
                          (Bm)              E7
He says,"The Yanks are coming, I can hear their rifles now."
     A                      D
He turns around in wonder, and what do you think he sees?
     A     D   E7          A
The Georg-i-a Militia eating goober peas.   Chorus


     A                      D              A
I think my song has lasted almost long enough,
                          (Bm)              E7
The subject's interesting but the rhymes are mighty rough,
     A                      D
I wish the war was over—when free from rags and fleas,
     A          D         E7          A
We'd kiss our wives and sweethearts and gobble goober peas.  Chorus
</pre>

# Folk Songs à la Mode

## Modal and Pentatonic Melodies

The term "mode" may be used interchangeably with "scale"—as in major mode or major scale, minor mode or minor scale. A scale is defined in terms of the intervals between its notes. A major scale has the following interval pattern:

To construct a major scale starting on any note, all you do is follow the above interval series.

There are three different types of minor scales.

Natural minor:

Harmonic minor:

Melodic minor:

These four scales (major and minor) demonstrate that the interval pattern between the fixed octave points may vary. There are other scales—modes—with other interval patterns which are of great importance to musicians. We shall consider a few of them here.

## The Dorian Mode

The Dorian mode is usually illustrated as starting on D. This is because on a piano it would comprise only the white keys and is easier to visualize that way. It starts out sounding like D minor because of the half step between the second and third notes, but in its last four notes (*tetrachord*) it presents an entirely new pattern.

It is, of course, possible to start a Dorian scale on any note—for example, A. All that is necessary is to maintain the correct pattern.

A song in the Dorian mode built upon A would have for its tonic chord *A minor*. In a strict harmonization of the song—that is, a harmonization utilizing only the notes of the Dorian mode—the dominant chord would be *G major*.

Try the following rhythmic pattern.

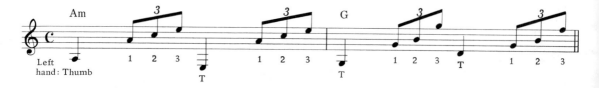

88

# What Shall We Do With The Drunken Sailor

                    Am
Chorus: Hooray, and up she rises,

            G
          Hooray, and up she rises,

            Am
          Hooray, and up she rises,

            G            Am
          Earlye in the morning.


            Am
          Put him in a long boat till he's sober,

            G
          Put him in a long boat till he's sober,

            Am
          Put him in a long boat till he's sober,

            G            Am
          Earlye in the morning.  *Chorus*


            Am
          Hang him by the leg in a running bowline,

            G
          Hang him by the leg in a running bowline,

            Am
          Hang him by the leg in a running bowline,

            G            Am
          Earlye in the morning.  *Chorus*


            Am
          Put him in the scuppers with a hose pipe on him,

            G
          Put him in the scuppers with a hose pipe on him,

            Am
          Put him in the scuppers with a hose pipe on him,

            G            Am
          Earlye in the morning.  *Chorus*


            Am
          Shave his belly with a rusty razor,

            G
          Shave his belly with a rusty razor,

            Am
          Shave his belly with a rusty razor,

            G            Am
          Earlye in the morning.  *Chorus*

<pre>
Am
That's what we'll do with the drunken sailor,

 G
That's what we'll do with the drunken sailor,

 Am
That's what we'll do with the drunken sailor,

 G              Am
Earlye in the morning.   *Chorus*
</pre>

Not all melodies in the Dorian mode need be harmonized strictly within
the mode—that is, utilizing chords made up only of notes of the scale.
Depending on the nature of the piece, the arranger should be free to make
his harmonization as interesting as possible.

Before turning to *She's like a Swallow* let us examine a useful arpeggio
in three-quarter time.

When the chord changes on the third beat . . .

# She's Like A Swallow

```
      Am      E7            Am
Down  to  this garden this fair maid did go,

      D       F      Am     Em
To pluck the beautiful prim-a-rose.

        F         G7        C        Am
The more she plucked, the more she pulled,

        Em      D E7  Am
Until she got her apron full.



      Am      E7            Am
Then out of these prim-a-roses she made

      D    F    Am      Em
A thorny pillow for her head.

        F          G7        C       Am
She laid her head down, no word did say,

              Em          D   E7   Am
And then this poor maid's heart did break.
```

*Repeat Verse One.*


## The Mixolydian Mode

The Mixolydian mode is usually illustrated as the G to G scale on the piano, utilizing only the white keys. It starts out sounding like *G major,* but its upper tetrachord gives it its characteristic sound.

Starting on D, we can construct the following Mixolydian scale.

A characteristic cadence in "Mixolydian D" involves the *D major* and *C major* chords. Play the following brush-stroke pattern.

93

In order to be able to play the melody of *Old Joe Clark* using this brush stroke, it is necessary to change the customary fingering of the *D major* chord.

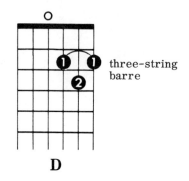

**D**

three-string
barre

## Old Joe Clark

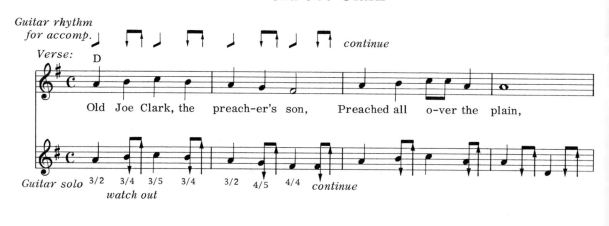

fol - low me ten thou-sand miles To hear my fid - dle play.

<table>
<tr><td>

D
I used to live on the mountain top,

But now I live in town,

I'm boarding at the big hotel,
        C      D
Courting Betsy Brown. *Chorus*

</td><td>

D
Old Joe had a yellow cat,

She would not sing or pray.

She stuck her head in a buttermilk jar
        C      D
And washed her sins away. *Chorus*

</td></tr>
</table>

D
Wish I was a sugar tree,

Standing in the town.

Every time a pretty girl passed,
      C     D
I'd shake some sugar down. *Chorus*

D
Old Joe Clark, he had a house,

Fifteen storeys high,

And every story in that house
      C     D
Was filled with chicken pie. *Chorus*

D
Wish I had my own sweetheart,

I'd set her on a shelf,

And every time she smiled at me,
      C     D
I'd get up there myself. *Chorus*

A two-octave scale in the Mixolydian mode starting on E:

The cadence with a brush stroke.

Count:  1    2    3    4    1    2    3    4

## Little Maggie

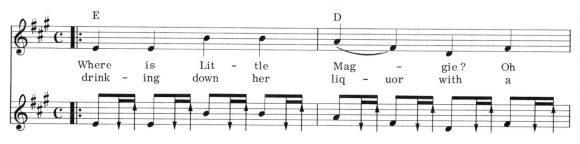

Where   is   Lit - tle   Mag - gie?   Oh
drink - ing   down   her   liq - uor   with   a

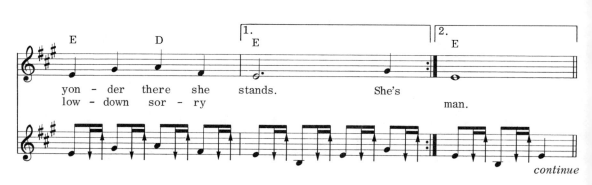

yon - der   there   she   stands.   She's
low - down   sor - ry                man.

*continue*

E              D
How can I just stand it,

E          D        E
To see those two blue eyes.

                      D
They're shining like two diamonds,

E          D        E
Two diamonds in the sky.


E              D
Sometimes I have a nickel,

E          D        E
Sometimes I have a dime.

                D
Sometimes I have ten dollars,

E          D        E
Just to buy little Maggie wine.


E                D
She's marching to the station,

E        D        E
Got a suitcase in her hand.

                D
She's going for to leave me,

E              D        E
She's bound for some distant land.


E                        D
Pretty flowers were made for blooming,

E          D        E
Pretty stars were made to shine.

                        D
Pretty girls were made for boys to love,

E            D        E
Little Maggie was made for mine.

96

```
        E                    D
The first time I seen Little Maggie,

         E              D        E
She was sitting by the banks of the sea,

                                       D
Had a forty-five strapped 'round her shoulder,

       E     D      E
And a banjo on her knee.
```

The Mixolydian scale starting on A.

A three-quarter-time arpeggio.

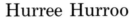

## Hurree Hurroo

Scottish Folk Song

97

one, And will you come a - way, _____ my

love, _____ To be my own, my

fair_____ one?

     A           G  
Smiling the land, smiling the sea,

     A                      D  A  
Sweet was the smell of the heather.

    D            A                D  
Would we were yonder, just you and me,

      A     G    A G A  
The two of us together. *Chorus*


     A             G  
All the day long out by the peat,

     A                   D  A  
Then by the shore in the gloaming.

    D           A               D  
Tripping it lightly with dancing feet,

      A     G    A G A  
Then we together roaming. *Chorus*

## The Phrygian Mode

The incidence of songs in this mode in American folk music is compara-
tively rare. It is to be found extensively in Spanish music (see *Ay! Linda
Amiga,* page 151)

Songs harmonized in the Phrygian mode present a somewhat ambiguous
tonality—in this case varying from *E minor* to *C major.*

## The Pentatonic Mode

The Pentatonic mode is very commonly employed in folk music the
world over. It is particularly widespread in music of the British Isles and
West Africa. The influence of the music of these two locales upon American folk music has been tremendous.

A characteristic of pentatonic scales is the avoidance of the half-step
interval and, of course, the five-note sequence.

Here is a pentatonic scale starting on *D.*

# Volga Boatman

Russain Folk Song

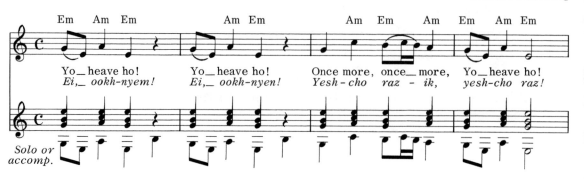

Yo__ heave ho! Yo__ heave ho! Once more, once__ more, Yo__ heave ho!
*Ei,__ ookh-nyem! Ei,__ ookh-nyen! Yesh-cho raz - ik, yesh-cho raz!*

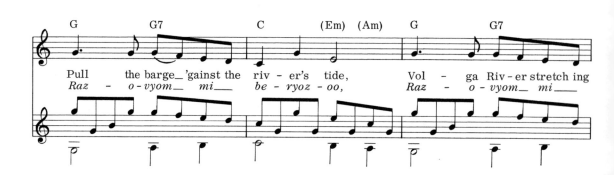

Pull the barge__ 'gainst the riv - er's tide, Vol - ga Riv - er stretch ing
*Raz - o-vyom__ mi__ be - ryoz - oo, Raz - o-vyom__ mi__*

far and wide. Ai da da, ai da, Ai da da, ai da,
*koo - driav - oo. Ai da da, ai da, Ai da da, ai da,*

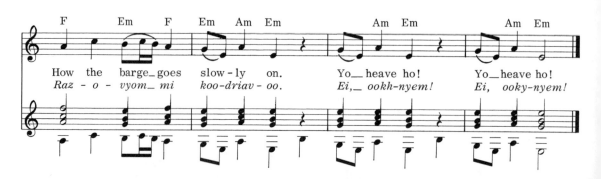

How the barge__ goes slow - ly on. Yo__ heave ho! Yo__ heave ho!
*Raz - o - vyom__ mi koo-driav - oo. Ei,__ ookh-nyem! Ei, ooky-nyem!*

100

Em  Am  Em        Am  Em
Yo, heave ho!  Yo, heave ho!

        Am    Em  Am  Em  Am  Em
Once more, once more, yo, heave ho!

G     G7      C    Em  Am
As the barges float along,

G       G7        C
To the sun we sing our song.

Am        Em
Ai  da da,  ai  da,

F          Em
Ai  da da,  ai  da,

F     Em  F  Em  Am  Em
To the sun we sing our song.

    Am  Em        Am  Em
Yo, heave ho!  Yo, heave ho!

Em  Am  Em        Am  Em
Yo, heave ho!  Yo, heave ho!

        Am    Em  Am  Em  Am  Em
Once more, once more, yo, heave ho!

G     G7      C    Em  Am
Volga, Volga our pride,

G       G7          C
Mighty stream so deep and wide.

Am        Em
Ai  da da,  ai  da,

F          Em
Ai  da da,  ai  da,

F     Em  F  Em  Am  Em
Mighty stream so deep and wide.

    Am  Em        Am  Em
Yo, heave ho!  Yo, heave ho!


Em  Am  Em        Am  Em
Ei, ookhnyem! Ei, ookhnyem!

      Am  Em Am Em Am  Em
Yeshcho razik, yeshcho raz!

  G     G7      C    Em  Am
Razovyom mi beryozoo,

  G     G7      C
Razovyom mi koodriavoo.

Am        Em
Ai  da da,  ai  da,

F          Em
Ai  da da,  ai  da,

  F    Em   F  Em  Am  Em
Razovoym mi koodriavoo.

    Am  Em        Am  Em
Ei, ookhnyem! Ei, ookhnyem!


Em  Am    Em      Am  Em
Ei, ookhnyem! Ei, ookhnyem!

      Am  Em Am Em Am  Em
Yeshcho razik, yeshcho raz!

G     G7      C    Em  Am
Mi po berezhkoo idyom,

G       G7        C
Pyesniu solnishkoo poyom.

Am        Em
Ai  da da,  ai  da,

F          Em
Ai  da da,  ai  da,

  F     Em  F  Em  Am  Em
Pyesniu solnishkoo poyom.

    Am  Em        Am  Em
Ei, ookhnyem! Ei, ookhnyem!


Em  Am    Em      Am  Em
Ei, ookhnyem! Ei, ookhnyem!

      Am  Em Am Em Am  Em
Yeshcho razik, yeshcho raz!

G       G7      C    Em  Am
Ekh, ti, Volga, mat-reka,

G     G7      C
Shiroka i glooboka

Am        Em
Ai  da da,  ai  da,

F          Em
Ai  da da,  ai  da,

  F    Em  F   Em Am Em
Shiroka  i  glooboka.

    Am  Em        Am  Em
Ei, ookhnyem! Ei, ookhnyem!

The characteristic harmonic feeling of this mode is not unlike the Dorian mode up to a point—the difference being that the notes F and B are not present in the scale.

## Shady Grove

Shad-y Grove, my lit-tle love, Shad-y Grove I say.

pull off       hammer on

Shad-y Grove, my lit-tle love, Bound for Shad-y Grove.

Dm      C
Wish I was in Shady Grove,

Dm     C    Dm
Sittin' in a rockin' chair,

   Am          C
And if those blues would bother me

Dm    C     Dm
I'd rock away from there. *Chorus*

Dm      C
Had a banjo made of gold,

Dm     C     Dm
Every string would shine.

   Am        C
The only song that it would play

Dm    C     Dm
Wish that girl was mine. *Chorus*

Dm      C
When I was in Shady Grove,

Dm     C     Dm
Heard them pretty birds sing.

   Am        C
The next time I go to Shady Grove,

Dm     C     Dm
Take along a diamond ring. *Chorus*

Dm      C
When you go to catch a fish,

Dm     C     Dm
Fish with a hook and line.

   Am        C
When you go to court a girl,

Dm    C    Dm
Never look behind. *Chorus*

Dm   C
When I was a little boy

Dm  C    Dm
All I wanted was a knife.

Am    C
Now I am a great big boy,

 Dm  C  Dm
I'm lookin' for a wife. *Chorus*

Often melodies in the Pentatonic mode blur the line between major and minor. The two following scales—in reality composed of the same notes—evoke *A minor* and *C major* feelings, respectively.

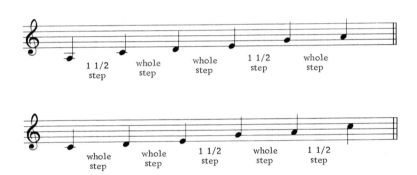

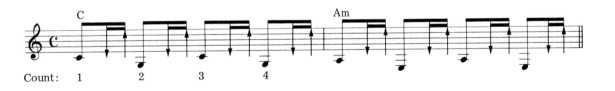

# Red Apple Juice

C        Am
Who'll rock the cradle, who'll sing this song,

C           Am
Who'll rock the cradle when I'm gone, Lord, Lord?

C   (G)     C
Who'll rock the cradle when I'm gone?


C        Am
I'll rock the cradle, I'll sing this song,

C         Am
I'll rock the cradle when you're gone, Lord, Lord.

C   (G)     C
I'll rock the cradle when you're gone.

```
      C                 Am
I've done all I can do, done all I can say,
C                   Am
I  can't go on this-a way, no, no.
C         (G)        C
I  can't go  on  this-a way.



      C                 Am
I've done all I can do, done all I can say,
     C                          Am
I'll sing it to your mama next payday, Lord, Lord.
     C        (G)           C
I'll sing it to your mama next payday.
```

It is possible for pentatonic melodies to be harmonized as if they were in major keys. Here is another pentatonic scale, starting on D—but with a different arrangement of intervals from that of *Shady Grove*.

We will write out the accompaniment in eighth notes as follows;

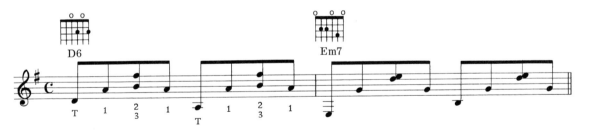

For *Bury Me Not on the Lone Prairie* the arpeggio assumes a "rocking" quality—triplets instead of eighths.

# Bury Me Not On The Lone Prairie

D6
*Chorus:* "Oh, bury me not on the lone prairie,
       Em7       D6
Where the wild coyotes will howl o'er me,

In a narrow grave just six by three.
       Em7       D6
Oh, bury me not on the lone prairie."

         D6
"It matters not, I've oft been told,

           Em7                            D6
Where the body lies when the heart grows cold.

Yet grant, oh grant this wish to me:
           Em7               D6
Oh, bury me not on the lone prairie." *Chorus*


          D6
"I've always wished to be laid when I died

             Em7               D6
In the little churchyard on the green hillside.

By my father's grave there let mine be,
           Em7              D6
And bury me not on the lone prairie." *Chorus*


          D6
"Oh, bury me not"—and his voice failed there,

           Em7            D6
But we took no heed of his dying prayer.

In a narrow grave just six by three
           Em7             D6
We buried him there on the lone prairie. *Chorus*


          D6
And the cowboys now as they roam the plain,

             Em7                 D6
For they marked the spot where his bones were lain,

Fling a handful of roses o'er his grave
           Em7               D6
With a prayer to Him who his soul will save. *Chorus*

SECTION FOUR

# Barre Chords

We need now to increase our chord vocabulary and our left-hand mobility. A good way to accomplish these desirable ends is with barre chords. When a finger of the left hand plays more than one string at a time in a given chord, that chord is a barre chord.

Lay your index finger across all six strings at the first fret. Press down firmly without arching the finger so that all six strings sound clearly. You may have to lower your wrist a bit more than usual in order to maintain the proper pressure.

With your remaining fingers play what would have been an *E major* chord if your first finger (the barre) were the nut (that is, the point at which the fingerboard begins). It is an *F major* chord. In this and all the following diagrams we will use a solid black line to indicate the index-finger barre.

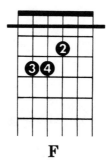

**F**

Use the brush stroke and the barre F.

## Bury Me Beneath The Willow

Bur - y me be - neath the wil - low, 'Neath the

108
108

weep-ing wil-low tree. _____ When he hears his _____ love is sleep-ing, May - be then he'll think of me. _____

C     F
My heart is sad and I am lonely
C     G7
Thinking of the one I love.
  C    F
When will I meet him? Oh, no never,
 C G7    C
Unless we meet in heaven above. *Chorus*

  C    F
Tomorrow was to be our wedding,
 C      G7
I pray, oh Lord, where can he be?
  C    F
He's gone, he's gone to love some other.
C G7    C
He no longer cares for me. *Chorus*

  C    F
He told me that he dearly loved me,
 C      G7
How could I believe him untrue?
  C    F
Until one day some neighbors told me,
 C G7    C
"He has proven untrue to you." *Chorus*

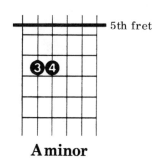

**A minor**

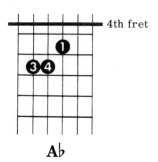

**A♭**

Use the following arpeggio. Try and get all of the notes of the barre chords to sound clearly.

## Jacob's Ladder

We are climb-ing  Ja - cob's lad - der,  We are climb-ing  Ja - cob's lad - der,

We are climb-ing  Ja - cob's lad - der,  Chil - dren  of  the  Lord.

C
Every rung goes higher and higher,
G7                              C
Every rung goes higher and higher,
Am      A♭        F        C
Every rung goes higher and higher,
        G7      C
Children of the Lord.


C
Every new man makes us stronger,
G7                              C
Every new man makes us stronger,

Am      A♭        F        C
Every new man makes us stronger,
        G7      C
Children of the Lord.

C
We have toiled in dark and danger,
G7                              C
We have toiled in dark and danger,
Am      A♭        F        C
We have toiled in dark and danger,
        G7      C
Children of the Lord. *Repeat Verse (*

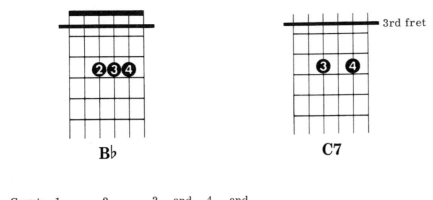

## The Wabash Cannonball

*Verse:*

I stood on the At - lan - tic O - cean, On the
long and she's tall and hand - some, Yes, she's

wide Pa - ci - fic shore, Saw the queen of flow - ing riv - ers, Might-y
loved by one and all, She's a mod - ern com - bi - na - tion Called the

1.
moun - tains by the score. She's

2.
Wa - bash Can - non - ball.

F
*Chorus:* Listen to the jingle,

Bb
The rumble and the roar.

C7
Riding through the woodlands,

F
To the hills and by the shore.

Hear the mighty rush of the engine,

Bb
Hear the lonesome hobo squall,

C7
Riding through the jungles

F
On the Wabash Cannonball.

F
Now, the eastern states are dandies,

Bb
So the western people say.

C7
From New York to St. Louis

F
And Chicago by the way.

Through the hills of Minnesota

Bb
Where the rippling waters fall,

C7
No chances can be taken

F
On the Wabash Cannonball. *Chorus*

F
Here's to Daddy Claxton,

Bb
May his name forever stand.

C7
May he ever be remembered

F
Through parts of all our land.

When his earthly race is over

Bb
And the curtain 'round him falls,

C7
We'll carry him to Glory

F
On the Wabash Cannonball. *Chorus*

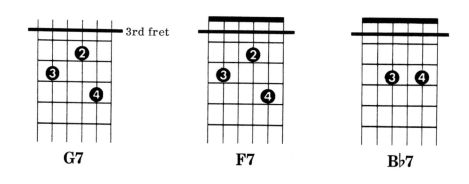

G7    F7    Bb7

# No Hiding Place

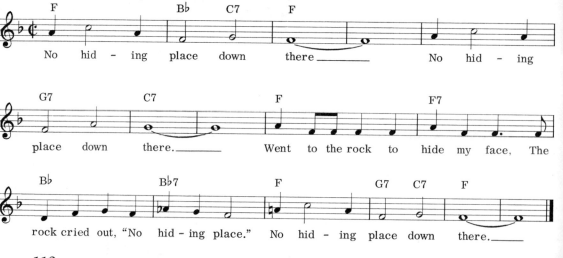

No hid - ing place down there _____ No hid - ing place down there. _____ Went to the rock to hide my face, The rock cried out, "No hid - ing place." No hid - ing place down there. _____

```
         F               Bb  C7  F
The rock cried, "I'm burning too."
                         G7      C7
The rock cried, "I'm burning too."
         F               F7
The rock cried out, "I'm burning too,
  Bb                          Bb7
I want to go to heaven the same as you,
         F       G7    C7   F
There's no hiding place down here."
```

```
    F               Bb       C7  F
Sinner man he stumbled and fell.
            G7              C7
Sinner man he stumbled and fell.
         F                   F7
Oh, the sinner man stumbled and he fell,
  Bb                              Bb7
Wanted to go to heaven but he had to go to hell,
         F       G7    C7   F
There's no hiding place down here.
```

*Repeat Verse One.*

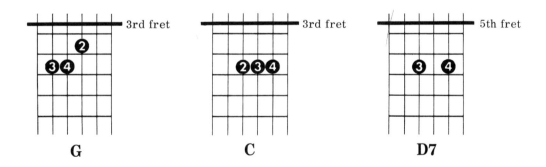

# Pick A Bale Of Cotton

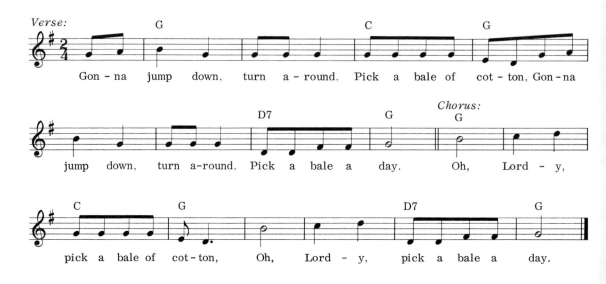

*Verse:*
Gon-na jump down, turn a-round, Pick a bale of cot-ton, Gon-na jump down, turn a-round, Pick a bale a day. Oh, Lord-y,

*Chorus:*
pick a bale of cot-ton, Oh, Lord-y, pick a bale a day.

    G                       C         G
I believe to my soul I can pick a bale of cotton,
                             D7        G
I believe to my soul I can pick a bale a day. *Chorus*

    G                       C         G
Me and my partner can pick a bale of cotton,
                            D7        G
Me and my partner can pick a bale a day. *Chorus*

    G                        C         G
Had a little woman who could pick a bale of cotton,
                            D7        G
Had a little woman who could pick a bale a day. *Chorus*

         G                      C
Gonna pick a, pick a, pick a, pick a, pick a bale of cotton,
    G                      D7     G
Gonna pick a, pick a, pick a, pick a, pick a bale a day. *Chorus*

# Worried Man Blues

*Chorus:*

It takes a wor-ried man to sing a wor-ried song, It takes a wor-ried man to sing a wor-ried song, It takes a wor-ried man to sing a wor-ried song, I'm wor-ried now,____ But I won't be wor-ried long.

      G
I went across the river and I lay down to sleep,
   C                                  G
I went across the river and I lay down to sleep,

I went across the river and I lay down to sleep,
           D7                     G
When I awoke I had shackles on my feet. *Chorus*

      G
Twenty-nine links of chain around my leg,
   C                                  G
Twenty-nine links of chain around my leg,

Twenty-nine links of chain around my leg,
           D7                     G
And on each link the initial of my name. *Chorus*

  G
I asked the judge what might be my fine,
C                                    G
I asked the judge what might be my fine,

I asked the judge what might be my fine,
          D7                                  G
Twenty-one years on the Rocky Mountain Line. *Chorus*

```
     G
Twenty-one years to pay my awful crime,
  C                                    G
Twenty-one years to pay my awful crime,

Twenty-one years to pay my awful crime,
              D7                   G
Twenty-one years—but I got ninety-nine.  Chorus
```

```
        G
The train arrived, sixteen coaches long,
  C                              G
The train arrived, sixteen coaches long,

The train arrived, sixteen coaches long,
              D7                 G
The girl I love is on that train and gone.  Chorus
```

```
      G
I looked down the track as far as I could see,
  C                                  G
I looked down the track as far as I could see,

I looked down the track as far as I could see,
              D7                     G
Little bitty hand was a-waving after me.  Chorus
```

```
      G
If anyone should ask you who composed this song,
  C                                      G
If anyone should ask you who composed this song,

If anyone should ask you who composed this song,
              D7                       G
Tell him it was I, and I sing it all day long.  Chorus
```

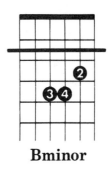

**Bminor**

## Bowling Green

Wish I was in Bowl-ing Green, sit-ting in a chair,

One arm 'round my pret-ty lit-tle miss, The oth-er 'round my

dear, The oth-er 'round my dear, Bowl-ing Green,_____

_____ Hey,_____ good old Bowl-ing Green._____

```
D                                                 Bm
If you see that gal of mine, tell her once for me,
D                        A7          D
If she loves another boy, yes, I'll set her free,
A7          D          Bm
Yes, I'll set her free, Bowling Green,
 D   A7              D
Hey, good old Bowling Green.
```

```
 D                                            Bm
Wish I was a bumblebee, sailing through the air,
D                                  A7          D
Sail right down to my true love's side, touch her if you dare,
 A7          D          Bm
Touch her if you dare, Bowling Green,
 D   A7              D
Hey, good old Bowling Green.
```

```
D                                                       Bm
Going through this whole wide world, I'm going through alone,
D                                      A7          D
Going through this whole wide world, I ain't got no home,
A7          D          Bm
I  ain't got no home, Bowling Green,
 D   A7              D
Hey, good old Bowling Green.
```

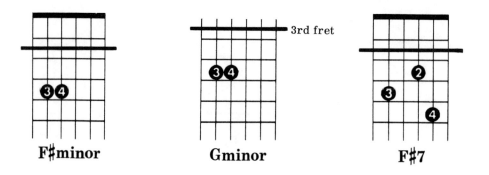

F♯minor          Gminor          F♯7

# Home In That Rock

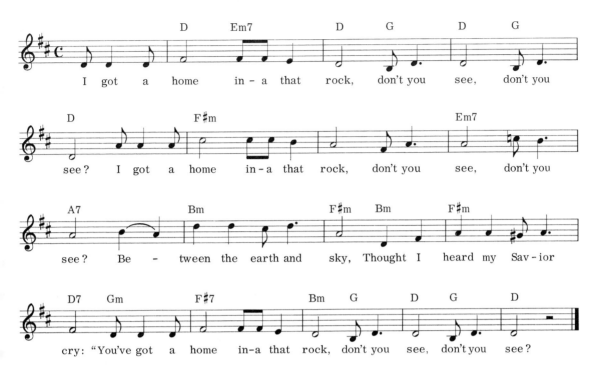

I got a home in-a that rock, don't you see, don't you see? I got a home in-a that rock, don't you see, don't you see? Be - tween the earth and sky, Thought I heard my Sav-ior cry: "You've got a home in-a that rock, don't you see, don't you see?

         D       Em7    D  G      D     G      D
Poor man Lazarus, poor as I, don't you see? Don't you see?
         F♯m                     Em7           A7
Poor man Lazarus, poor as I, don't you see? Don't you see?
        Bm             F♯m
Poor man Lazarus, poor as I,
  Bm     F♯m                  D7
When he died he found a home on high,
Gm      F♯7           Bm  G      D     G      D
He had a home in-a that rock, don't you see? Don't you see?


          D      Em7    D  G      D     G      D
Rich man Dives lived so well, don't you see? Don't you see?
         F♯m                    Em7           A7
Rich man Dives lived so well, don't you see? Don't you see?
        Bm           F♯m
Rich man Dives lived so well,
  Bm     F♯m                  D7
When he died he found a home in hell,
Gm      F♯7          Bm  G      D     G      D
Had no home in-a that rock, don't you see? Don't you see?

```
       D        Em7     D    G      D    G      D
God gave Noah the rainbow sign, don't you see? Don't you see?
       F#m                                Em7              A7
God gave Noah the rainbow sign, don't you see? Don't you see?
       Bm               F#m
God gave Noah the rainbow sign,

Bm        F#m                  D7
No more water—but fire next time,

Gm           F#7           Bm    G      D    G      D
Noah had a home in-a that rock, don't you see? Don't you see?
```

*Repeat Verse One.*

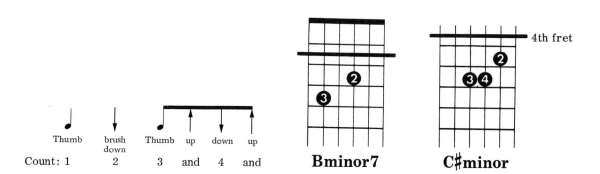

Count: 1    2    3  and  4  and        **Bminor7**     **C#minor**

## Union Train

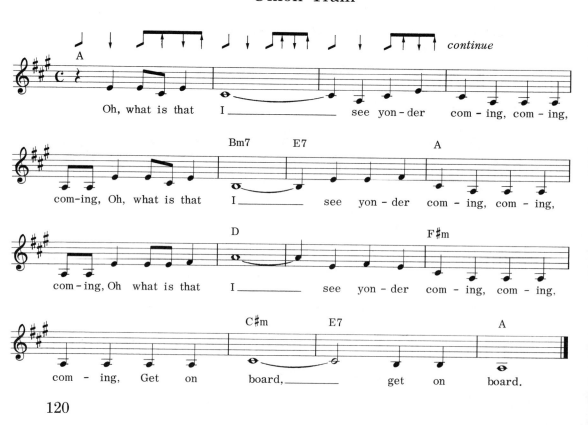

Oh, what is that I _____ see yon-der com-ing, com-ing,

com-ing, Oh, what is that I_____ see yon-der com-ing, com-ing,

com-ing, Oh what is that I_____ see yon-der com-ing, com-ing,

com-ing, Get on board,_____ get on board.

```
                A
It's that union train a-coming, coming, coming,

        Bm7 E7              A
It's that  u - union train a-coming, coming, coming,

        D           F♯m
It's that union train a-coming, coming, coming,

        C♯m E7          A
Get on board,    get on board.



                A
It has saved a-many a thousand, thousand, thousand,

        Bm7 E7          A
It has saved   a-many a thousand, thousand, thousand,

        D           F♯m
It has saved a-many a thousand, thousand, thousand,

        C♯m E7            A
Get on board,    get on board.



            A
It will carry us to freedom, freedom, freedom,

        Bm7 E7        A
It will  carry us to freedom, freedom, freedom,

        A         F♯m
It will carry us to freedom, freedom, freedom,

        C♯m E7          A
Get on board,    get on board.



            A
It will carry us to vict'ry, vict'ry, vict'ry,

        Bm7 E7        A
It will  carry us to vict'ry, vict'ry, vict'ry,

        D           F♯m
It will carry us to  vict'ry, vict'ry, vict'ry,

        C♯m E7          A
Get on board,    get on board.



            A
Let us join the one big union, union, union,

        Bm7 E7            A
Let us join    the one big union, union, union,

        D               F♯m
Let us join the one big  union, union, union,

        C♯m E7            A
Get on board,    get on board.
```

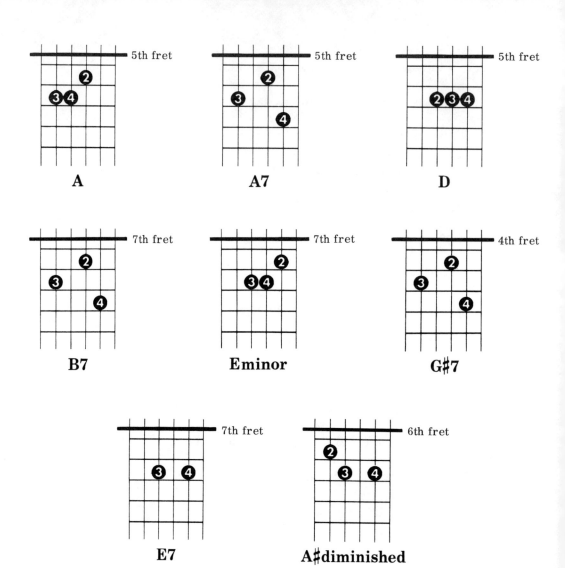

# The Panic Is On

What this coun-try is com-ing to___ some_ would like to know.

If they don't do some-thing bye and bye,___ The rich will live and the

poor_ will die,___ Dog - gone, I mean the pan - ic is

on.___ on.___

    A       A7       D     D7
Can't get work, can't draw no pay,

B7             Em
Unemployment's worser every day.

    A       A7       D     G♯7
Nothing to eat, no place to sleep,

    A     C♯m        F♯7
All night long folks are walking the street.

    B7   E7             A
Doggone—I mean the panic is on.


       A       A7         D      D7
Saw a man this morning, walking down the street

B7             Em
In his B. V. D. s, no shoes on his feet.

     A      A7   D    G♯7
You oughta seen the women in their flats,

       A   C♯m           F♯7
You could hear 'em saying, "What kinda man is that?"

    B7   E7            A  A♯dim  B7  E7
Doggone—I mean the panic is on.

```
 A         A7              D        D7
All them landlords done raised the rent.

 B7                    Em
Folks that ain't broke is badly bent.

 A                     A7         D        G#7
Where they gets the dough from, goodness knows,

          A      C#m          F#7
But if they don't produce it—in the street they go.

 B7      E7                        A
 Doggone—I mean the panic is on.


 A         A7              D        D7
Some play numbers, some read your mind,

 B7                    Em
They all got a racket of some kind.

 A                 A7         D     G#7
Some trimming corns offa people's feet,

        A      C#m          F#7
They gotta do something to make ends meet.

 B7      E7                        A   A#dim  B7   E7
 Doggone—I mean the panic is on.


       A         A7       D        D7
Some women selling apples, some selling pie,

 B7                    Em
Some selling gin and rye.

 A                 A7          D     G#7
Some are selling socks to support their man,

       A          C#m          F#7
In fact, some are selling everything they can.

 B7      E7                        A
 Doggone—I mean the panic is on.


       A         A7          D        D7
I've pawned my clothes, pawned my everything,

 B7                    Em
Pawned my jewelry, my watch and ring.

 A         A7        D     G#7
Pawned my razor but not my gun,

        A      C#m                     F#7
So if luck don't change, there'll be some stealing done.

 B7      E7                        A   A#dim  B7   E7
 Doggone—I mean the panic is on.
```

```
    A         A7              D      D7
Old Prohibition's ruined everything,

    B7                Em
That's why I must sing.

    A         A7              D      G#7
Here's one thing I want you all to hear:

              A         C#m        F#7
Till they bring back light wine, gin and beer,

    B7      E7                          A
Doggone—the panic will be on.
```

G#minor

## Deep Blue Sea

Deep   blue   sea,   ba - by,   deep   blue   sea.

Deep   blue   sea,   ba - by,   deep   blue   sea.   Deep   blue

sea,   ba - by,   deep   blue   sea.   It   was   Wil - lie

*pluck chords*

what   got   drown-ded   in   the   deep   blue   sea.

```
  E  F♯m  E         A        E              E   F♯m  E          A        E
Dig his grave with a silver spade,        Lower him down with a golden chain,
    F♯m G♯m C♯m  F♯m F♯7  B7                  F♯m  E            F♯m F♯7 B7
Dig his grave with a silver spade,        Lower him down with a golden chain,
  E  F♯m  E         A        E              E   F♯m  E          A        E
Dig his grave with a silver spade,        Lower him down with a golden chain,

It was Willie what got drownded          It was Willie what got drownded
A  Am   E   B7   E                       A  Am   E   B7   E
In the deep blue sea.                    In the deep blue sea.
```

```
          E  F♯m  E          A        E
        Golden   sun bring him back again,
            F♯m  E               F♯m F♯7 B7
        Golden   sun bring him back  again,
          E  F♯m  E          A        E
        Golden   sun bring him back again,

        It was Willie what got drownded
        A  Am   E   B7   E
        In the deep blue sea.
```

*Repeat Verse One.*

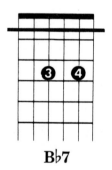

**Bb7**

## Don't Let Your Deal Go Down

Don't let your deal go down,_____ 'Til your

last gold dol - lar is gone.\_\_\_\_\_

E7 E♭7 D7 C♯7    F♯7
Well, I've been all around this whole wide world,

 B7    E
Done 'most everything.

E7 E♭7 D7 C♯7    F♯7
Well, I've played cards with the king and the queen,

  B7     E
The ace, the deuce and the trey. *Chorus*


E7 E♭7 D7  C♯7    F♯7
Where did you get that bright red dress,

   B7      E
And the shoes that you wear so fine?

E7 E♭7 D7 C♯7    F♯7
I got my dress and I got my shoes

    B7     E
From a driver down in the mine. *Chorus*


E7 E♭7 D7 C♯7     F♯7
I left my little girl a-crying,

 B7    E
Standing in the door.

E7 E♭7 D7 C♯7      F♯7
She throwed her arms all around my neck,

    B7     E
Saying, "Honey, please don't go." *Chorus*

## Major Chords

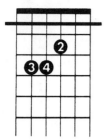

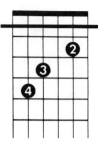

| Fret | Chord |
|------|-------|
| 1 | F |
| 2 | F♯/G♭ |
| 3 | G |
| 4 | G♯/A♭ |
| 5 | A |
| 6 | A♯/B♭ |
| 7 | B |
| 8 | C |
| 9 | C♯/D♭ |
| 10 | D |
| 11 | D♯/E♭ |
| 12 | E |

| Fret | Chord |
|------|-------|
| 1 | B♭/A♯ |
| 2 | B |
| 3 | C |
| 4 | C♯/D♭ |
| 5 | D |
| 6 | D♯/E♭ |
| 7 | E |
| 8 | F |
| 9 | F♯/G♭ |
| 10 | G |
| 11 | G♯/A♭ |
| 12 | A |

| Fret | Chord |
|------|-------|
| 1 | C♯/D♭ |
| 2 | D |
| 3 | D♯/E♭ |
| 4 | E |
| 5 | F |
| 6 | F♯/G♭ |
| 7 | G |
| 8 | G♯/A♭ |
| 9 | A |
| 10 | A♯/B♭ |
| 11 | B |
| 12 | C |

## Minor Chords

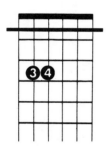

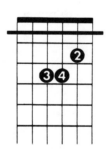

| Fret | Chord |
|------|-------|
| 1 | Fm |
| 2 | F♯m/G♭m |
| 3 | Gm |
| 4 | G♯m/A♭m |
| 5 | Am |
| 6 | A♯m/B♭m |
| 7 | Bm |
| 8 | Cm |
| 9 | C♯m/D♭m |
| 10 | Dm |
| 11 | D♯m/E♭m |
| 12 | Em |

| Fret | Chord |
|------|-------|
| 1 | B♭m/A♯m |
| 2 | Bm |
| 3 | Cm |
| 4 | C♯m/D♭m |
| 5 | Dm |
| 6 | D♯m/E♭m |
| 7 | Em |
| 8 | Fm |
| 9 | F♯m/G♭m |
| 10 | Gm |
| 11 | G♯m/A♭m |
| 12 | Am |

# Dominant Seventh Chords

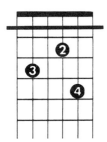

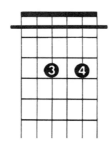

*Technically not a barre chord but still a useful movable chord. (Numbers refer to fret played by first finger. Do not play 6th and 1st strings.)*

| Fret | Chord |
|------|-------|
| 1 | F7 |
| 2 | F♯7/G♭7 |
| 3 | G7 |
| 4 | G♯7/A♭7 |
| 5 | A7 |
| 6 | A♯7/B♭7 |
| 7 | B7 |
| 8 | C7 |
| 9 | C♯7/D♭7 |
| 10 | D7 |
| 11 | D♯7/E♭7 |
| 12 | E7 |

| Fret | Chord |
|------|-------|
| 1 | B♭7/A♯7 |
| 2 | B7 |
| 3 | C7 |
| 4 | C♯7/D♭7 |
| 5 | D7 |
| 6 | D♯7/E♭7 |
| 7 | E7 |
| 8 | F7 |
| 9 | F♯7/G♭7 |
| 10 | G7 |
| 11 | G♯7/A♭7 |
| 12 | A7 |

| Fret | Chord |
|------|-------|
| 1 | C7 |
| 2 | C♯7/D7 |
| 3 | D7 |
| 4 | D♯7/E♭7 |
| 5 | E7 |
| 6 | F7 |
| 7 | F♯7/G♭7 |
| 8 | G7 |
| 9 | G♯7/A♭7 |
| 10 | A7 |
| 11 | A♯7/B♭7 |
| 12 | B7 |

# Minor Seventh Chords

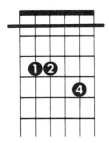

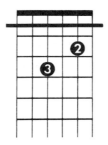

| Fret | Chord |
|------|-------|
| 1 | Fm7 |
| 2 | F♯m7/G♭m7 |
| 3 | Gm7 |
| 4 | G♯m7/A♭m7 |
| 5 | Am7 |
| 6 | A♯m7/B♭m7 |
| 7 | Bm7 |
| 8 | Cm7 |
| 9 | C♯m7/D♭m7 |
| 10 | Dm7 |
| 11 | D♯m7/E♭m7 |
| 12 | Em7 |

| Fret | Chord |
|------|-------|
| 1 | B♭m7/A♯m7 |
| 2 | Bm7 |
| 3 | Cm7 |
| 4 | C♯m7/D♭m7 |
| 5 | Dm7 |
| 6 | D♯m7/E♭m7 |
| 7 | Em7 |
| 8 | Fm7 |
| 9 | F♯m7/G♭m7 |
| 10 | Gm7 |
| 11 | G♯m7/A♭m7 |
| 12 | Am7 |

# Blues

It is in the area of blues that a folk guitarist really has an opportunity to come into his own. No longer is it sufficient for the guitar to serve as merely an accompaniment—it now emerges as an equal partner with the voice: A polished blues performance is a duet for voice and guitar.

The fundamental concepts of blues form and rhythm have been gone into in *How to Play the Guitar*. We shall begin here, more or less, where that volume left off—exploring the interworking between the vocal and instrumental parts.

## It Makes a Long-Time Man Feel Bad

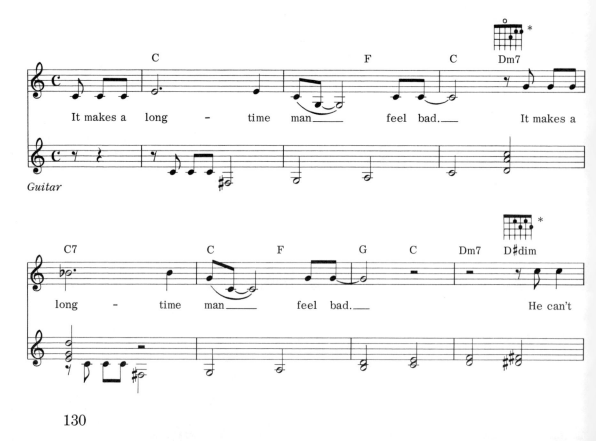

get      no   let-ter,_____ he can't   hear_____    from   home._____ It makes a

long   -   time   man__     feel   bad.__

*Chord diagrams are just for general information—read the music!

      C                      F     C  Dm7
Alberta, let your hair grow long,

      C7            C F      G  C  Dm7  D♯dim
Alberta, let your hair grow long,

             C      C7      F7          C-Am
Let it grow so long  till it drags to the ground.

      C                   F      C
Alberta, let your hair grow long.


           C            F       C
Well, surely my mother  must be gone,

        C7       C    F        G  C  Dm7  D♯dim
Well, surely my mother  must be gone,

        C     C7          F7      C-Am
Well, surely my mother must be gone, oh, Lord.

             C            F   C
It makes a long-time man  feel bad.


         C              F   C  Dm7
And I had five years  one time,

        C7      C F     G  C  Dm7  D♯dim
And I had five years  one time,

        C    C7       F7     C-Am
And I had five years one time, oh, Lord.

            C           F   C
But I rolled till I rolled it down.     *Repeat Verse One.*

The guitar part for *Chilly Winds* is syncopated three-finger picking with the very important addition of nonchordal tones and moving bass and treble lines. Examine each measure carefully. Don't just look at the chord name.

## Chilly Winds

*Guitar, repeat last two measures and fade out for ending.*

C                     F7                    C                 C7
I'm going where there ain't no ice and snow, darlin' baby,
   F7(9)                 Db7              C
I'm going where there ain't no ice and snow,
      Em7      G7          C
When I'm gone to my long lonesome home.


    C                   F7                 C                C7
I'm going where the folks all know my name, darlin' baby,
   F7(9)                Db7              C
I'm going where the folks all know my name,
      Em7      G7          C
When I'm gone to my long lonesome home.


     C       F7                 C              C7
I'm here in the jailhouse on my knees, darlin' baby,
   F7(9)       Db7              C
I'm here in the jailhouse on my knees,
      Em7      G7          C
When I'm gone to my long lonesome home.


   C       F7              C             C7
Make me a pallet on your floor, darlin' baby,
F7(9)      Db7             C
Make me a pallet on your floor,
     Em7      G7          C
When I'm gone to my long lonesome home.


     C        F7           C             C7
Now, who'll be your daddy when I'm gone, darlin' baby,
F7(9)      Db7         C
Who'll be your daddy when I'm gone,
     Em7      G7          C
When I'm gone to my long lonesome home?     *Repeat Verse One.*

133

The guitar part for *In the Pines* is an instrumental (melodic) solo played with a variation of the syncopated three-finger pattern.

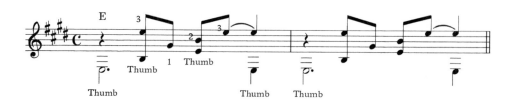

## In The Pines

```
        E           E7        A              C7
Tell me, where did you get them pretty little shoes,
         E           B7        E
And the dress you wear so fine?
          E7          A           C7
I got my dress from a railroad man,
          E           B7            E
Got my shoes from a driver in the mine.


    E           E7          A              C7
I wish to the Lord I'd-a never been born,
     E        B7        E
Or died when  I was young.
                 E7           A              C7
I never would have kissed your sweet, sweet lips,
        E           B7          E
Nor heard your rattling tongue.


       E       E7    A          C7
The longest train I ever did ride
          E       B7      E
Was a hundred coaches long.
           E7       A        C7
The only woman I ever did love,
         E      B7        E
She's on that train and gone.


      E             E7              A          C7
Them long steel rails and them short crossties
     E     B7      E
Ain't got no end, I know.
                  E7        A          C7
On these long steel rails and short crossties
        E          B7        E
I'm tramping my way back home.


    E            E7            A         C7
Longest old train in this whole wide world
          E          B7            E
Comes around Joe Brown's coal mine.
                E7         A          C7
Headlight comes 'round when the sun comes up,
         E            B7        E
The caboose when the sun goes down.
```

```
      E      E7     A      C7
Yes, my husband was a railroad man,
          E          B7              E
Was the best in this high lonesome world.
        E7          A          C7
The only thing that he did that was wrong
        E          B7        E
Was to miss just a-one little curve.


        E      E7     A      C7
My husband was a railroad man,
        E          B7        E
Killed a mile and a half from town.
          E7          A      C7
I found his head in an engine wheel,
        E          B7        E
But his body could never be found.


        E      E7              A              C7
True love, true love, tell me, where will you go?
        E          B7          E
I'm gonna go where the cold winds blow.
                E7          A              C7
I'm gonna weep, gonna cry, gonna moan, gonna sigh
        E          B7          E
Gonna dance in my good-time clothes.
```

*Repeat Verse One.*

Blues in three-quarter time are relatively rare. In order to play the melody of the *House of the Rising Sun,* the bass register is set off by a simple arpeggio.

## House Of The Rising Sun

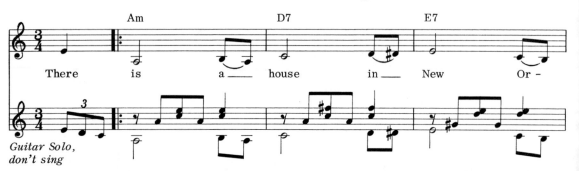

*Guitar Solo,
don't sing*

Am ... G7 ... C

leans, They call the Ris - ing Sun.

E7 ... Am ... Am7 ... Am6

It has been the ru-in of man-y a poor

F7 ... Am ... E7

girl, And I, oh Lord, was

1.
Am ... E7

one. If

Final ending
Am ... Am6

Sun.

Am      D7          E7  Am
If I had listened to what mama said,

        G7     C    E7
I'd 'a' been at home today.

Am      Am7    Am6          F7
Being so young and foolish, poor girl,

    Am     E7       Am  E7
Let a gambler lead me astray.

Am      D7      E7 Am
My mother, she's a tailor,

        G7              C - E7
She sells those new blue jeans.

    Am      Am7   Am6          F7
My sweetheart, he's a drunkard, Lord,

      Am     E7       Am E7
Drinks down in New Orleans.

137

     Am   D7    E7      Am
The  only thing a drunkard needs

           G7     C - E7
Is a suitcase and a trunk.

     Am  Am7    Am6  F7
The  only time he's  satisfied

      Am     E7   Am  E7
Is when he's  on a drunk.


      Am    D7    E7 Am
Go tell my baby, sister,

          G7       C - E7
Never do like  I  have done.

     Am     Am7     Am6     F7
To shun that house in New Orleans,

       Am    E7    Am  E7
They call the Rising Sun.

      Am   D7   E7 Am
One foot is  on the platform,

            G7      C - E7
And the other one  on the train.

     Am  Am7    Am6     F7
I'm going back to New Orleans

      Am     E7     Am  E7
To wear that ball and chain.


      Am    D7    E7      Am
I'm going back to New Orleans,

          G7     C - E7
My race is  almost run.

Am   Am7   Am6     F7
Going back to  end my life

     Am      E7    Am  Am6
Beneath the Rising Sun.

If you move a *B seventh* chord up one fret, you get a peculiar dissonant combination of notes. If it were not for the open B string, the chord would be *C seventh*. But it is precisely that note that gives it the blues quality. The function of this "C7" chord is to resolve back to the comparative consonance of the *B seventh* in the last measure to set up the repeat for the next verse. It is a very important bit of bluesy spice.

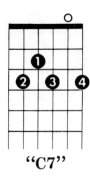

"C7"

Another approach to the playing of melody is by use of block chords and double stops (two notes played simultaneously).

## Been In The Pen So Long

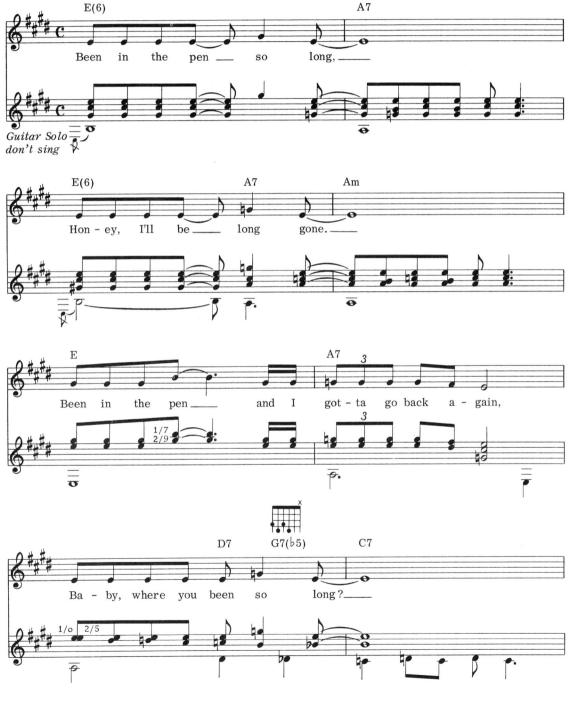

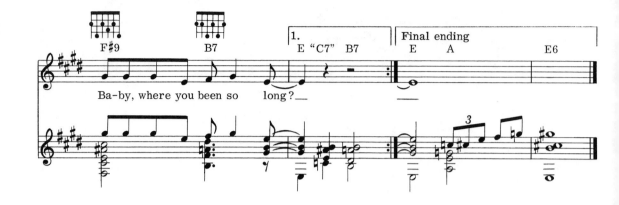

E(6)                                    A7
Awful lonesome, all alone and blue,

E(6)            A7            Am
Awful lonesome, all alone and blue,

 E                           A7
All alone and blue, no one to tell my troubles to,

              D7  G7(♭5) C7
Baby, where you been  so   long?

F♯9                B7        E    "C7" B7
Baby, where you been so long?


E(6)                                         A7
Some folks crave for Memphis, Tennessee,

E(6)                A7                Am
Some folks crave for Memphis, Tennessee,

 E                       A7
Some folks crave for Memphis, Tennessee,

              D7     G7(♭5)   C7
But New Orleans is good enough for me,

F♯9                B7                E   "C7" B7
New Orleans is good enough for me.

*Repeat Verse One.*

It is always effective to change registers—from high to low or low to high—in an instrumental solo.

## Alberta, Let Your Hair Hang Low

*Chord diagrams are not for the solo part. They may be used as part of a vocal accompaniment.

```
         Am           F7        Am - F7 - Am
Alberta, what's on your mind?
         C           G7        Cmaj7 - C7
Alberta, what's on your mind?
         F     F7 Em    E7          Am7 C7   Fmaj7 - Fm(maj7)
You keep me   worried,  bothered all   the time.
     C Gm6 A7      D7 G7       C  -  E7
Alberta,    what's on   your mind?


         Am           F7        Am - F7 - Am
Alberta, don'cha treat me unkind.
         C           G7        Cmaj7 - C7
Alberta, don'cha treat me unkind.
         F   F7   Em E7         Am7   C7   Fmaj7 - Fm(maj7)
Oh, my heart  is sad  'cause I want you   so bad.
     C Gm6 A7        D7    G7   C
Alberta,   don'cha treat me   unkind.
```

Use a down-up brush stroke for the accompaniment. Note the *"blues bass run"* and the *"break"* passages in the solo. These may be played both in the accompaniment and the solo.

## You Don't Know My Mind

C
You can't tell, you can't tell, you can't tell how I feel,          C7

F7(9)                                            C
You   can't tell, you can't tell how I feel,

C#dim          G7                    F7(9)              G7      C - F7(9) - C - G7
With   these cold iron shackles—shackles diggin' in my heel.


C
You can't see, you can't see, you can't see me now,          C7

F7(9)                                            C
You   can't see me, baby, you can't see me now,

C#dim      G7                F7(9)                  G7      C - F7(9) - C
'Cause I'm long-time gone—gone and won't be back nohow.

The blues arpeggio—written as eighth notes

and played as triplets.

Note the *"break"* and the *"blues bass run."*

## Betty And Dupree

*Chord diagrams for solo part.

A        E7   D7            A — A7
He said, "Lie down, little Betty, see what tomorrow brings."

    D7                 D♯dim    A
He said, "Lie down, little Betty, see what tomorrow brings.

  E7                   A D7 - A - E7
It may bring you sunshine, may bring you that diamond ring."


      A      E7    D7        A   A7
Then he got his pistol, went to the jewelry store,

  D7             D♯dim    A
He got his pistol, went to the jewelry store.

    E7                  A - D7 - A - E7
He killed a policeman and he wounded four or five more.

        A            E7         D7            A - A7
Then he went to the post office to get his evening mail,
  D7                         D♯dim   A
Went to the post office to get his evening mail,
  E7                                                   A - D7 - A - E7
Sheriff caught poor Dupree and put him in that old Atlanta jail.


          A           E7           D7                A   A7
Dupree's mother said to Betty, "Looka here what you done done."
    D7                  D♯dim     A
She said to Betty, "See what   you   done done.
         E7                                A - D7 - A - E7
Made my boy rob and steal and now he's gonna be hung."


          A          E7         D7         A - A7
"Give my daddy my clothes—poor Betty, give her my shoes,
         D7                          D♯dim    A
Give my daddy my clothes, give my baby, Betty, my shoes.
  E7                                      A - D7 - A - E7
If anybody asks you, say I died with the heartbreaking blues."


      A     E7    D7         A - A7
Sail on, sail on, sail on, Dupree, sail on.
    D7                   D♯dim     A
Sail on, sail on, sail on, Dupree,  sail on.
    E7                                   A - D7 - A7
You don't mind sailing, you'll be gone so doggone long.


# Things About Comin' My Way

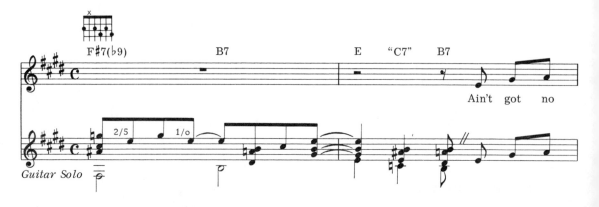

The pot was empty, the cupboard bare,

I said, "Mama, mama, what's goin' on here?" *Chorus*

The rent was due, the light was out,

I said, "Mama, mama, what's it all about?" *Chorus*

Sister was sick, doc wouldn't come

'Cause we couldn't pay him the proper sum. *Chorus*

147

```
              E                        E7
    Lost all my money, ain't got a dime,
A7                                          E
    Givin' up this cold world, leavin' it behind.   Chorus
```

```
              E                        E7
    Work all this summer and all the fall,
A7                                          E
    Gonna make this Christmas in my overalls.   Chorus
```

```
              E                        E7
    One of these days—it won't be long,
A7                                   E
    You'll call my name and I'll be gone.
```

```
Final              A7          E       Bm   C♯7
Chorus: 'Cause after all my hard trav'lin',
        F♯7(♭9)      B7       E   A7  E
        Things'll by comin' my way.
```

In order to achieve the effect of parallel octaves, we must tune the low
E string down one note to a still lower D.

Now the fourth and sixth strings are an octave apart. The melody is
now played simultaneously at the same fret on both strings. It may be
used as accompaniment and solo. For the chorus I have written out
separate parts for accompaniment and solo.

## Jerry

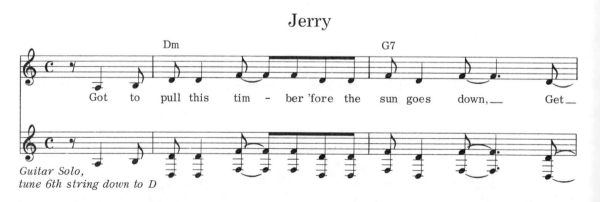
```
```

```
Dm                    G7
My old Jerry is an Arkansas mule,

 Dm                       G7      Dm
Been everywhere and he ain't no fool.

             G7          Dm
Work is heavy, old Jerry get sore;

 G7                           Dm
Pull so much and won't pull no more.   Chorus


Dm                       G7
Jerry's old shoulder is six feet tall,

 Dm                       G7        Dm
Pull more timber than a freight can haul.

             G7      Dm
Weighs nine hundred and twenty-two—

 G7                           Dm
Done everything a poor mule can do.   Chorus


 Dm                       G7
Boss hit Jerry and he made him jump,

Dm                        G7        Dm
Jerry reared and kicked the boss on the rump.

             G7      Dm
My old Jerry was a good old mule,

G7                                  Dm
Had it been me, Lord, I'd have killed that fool.   Chorus


 Dm                       G7
Boss tried to shoot old Jerry in the head,

Dm                            G7      Dm
Jerry ducked that bullet and he stomped him dead.

             G7      Dm
Stomped that boss till I wanted to scream,

 G7                                  Dm
Shoulda killed him 'cause he's so damn mean.   Chorus
```

# SECTION SIX

# Foreign and Far Out

The guitar, as you may have noticed by now, is a very versatile instrument. It is at home in a multitude of musical settings. In this section you will find some of its more exotic possibilities.

*Ay! Linda Amiga* is a typical Spanish folk song in that while it appears to be in *A minor* it is really in the Phrygian mode based on E. The Phrygian mode, you will remember, is made up of the natural notes from E to E. The one G sharp (in the next to the last measure) is merely a small "variation" from the strict Phrygian.

## Ay! Linda Amiga

Spanish Folk Song

Pe-na sin do-lor, Ni do-lor tan a-gu-do Co-mo el del a-
*Sor-row with-out pain, Nor a pain so in-tense as love's old sad re-*

mor, Ni do-lor tan a-gu-do Co-mo el del a-mor.
*frain, Nor a pain so in-tense as love's old sad re-frain.*

*D. C. al Fine*
*From the beginning*
*to "the end"*

Am    G    F    E
*Ah, dearest sweetheart, how proud and unbending*

Am  G   F    E
*Beautiful lady, my life you are ending.*

  Am   G   F
*No love without sorrow,*

  Am   G   F
*Sorrow without pain.*

  E  A A7 Dmsus4 Dm
*Nor pain so intense  as*

    G7   C
*Love's sad refrain.*

Am    G    F    E
*Ah, dearest sweetheart, how proud and unbending,*

Am  G   F    E
*Beautiful lady, my life you are ending.*

The first four measures of *Sano Duso* are based on a common Middle Eastern tetrachord.

The rest of the song is pure Phrygian with a tonic of C sharp.

# Sano Duso

Serbian Folk Song

1. Shano dusho
2. Oy

```
Dm              E
Noch li hodi divno, Sano,

Dm          E
Ja  si tuga vijem.

 Dm           E
Noch li hodi divno, Sano,

Dm            E
Ja  si tuga vijem.

D
Ubavinja tvoja, Sano,

E7              A Amaj7
Ne da mi da spijem.    Chorus
```

```
Dm                  E
Oh, the night is wond'rous, Shano,

Dm                  E
But my heart is aching.

Dm                  E
Oh, the night is wond'rous, Shano,

Dm                  E
But my heart is aching.

 D
How your beauty, my dear Shano,

 E7                A Amaj7
Keeps me ever waking.    Chorus
```

# Toom Balalaika

Jewish Folk Song

```
Am                          E
Narisher bocher, vos darfst du fregen,

   E7                          Am
A shteyn ken vaksn, vaksn ohn regn,

            Dm          Am
A liebe ken brennen oon nit oyfheren,

   Dm       E     E7        Am
A hartz ken beynken, veynen ohn treren.   Chorus
```

```
   Am                          E
Tell me, maiden, I'd like to know,

   E7                          Am
What it is needs no rain to grow.

                  Dm      Am
What's not consumed although it's burning?

   Dm          E     E7      Am
What weeps no tears although it's yearning?   Chorus
```

```
   Am                          E
You foolish boy, didn't you know,

   E7                          Am
A stone does not need rain to grow?

                  Dm      Am
A love's not consumed although it's burning,

   Dm          E     E7      Am
A heart weeps no tears although it's yearning.   Chorus
```

The next six songs have purposely not been translated. They all deal with aspects of love—its joys and sorrows—in German, Italian, French, and Russian. Give them a try in their native languages—the languages that inspired the composers of their music.

## Serenade

Words by
Rellstab

Music by
Franz Schubert
(1797-1828)

mir.
mich.

Flü - sternd schlan - ke Wip - fel rau - schen in __ des Mon - des
Sie ver - steh'n des Bu - sens Seh - nen, ken - nen Lie - bes-

Licht, in __ des Mon - des Licht,
schmerz, ken - nen Lie - bes-schmerz,

des Ver-rä - thers feind - lich Lau - schen fürch - te, Hol - de,
rüh - ren mit den Sil - ber-tö - nen je - des Wei - che

*2nd time to Coda*

nicht, fürch - te, Hol - de, nicht.
Herz, je - des Wei - che Herz.

159

*(Repeat for 2nd verse from the sign 𝄋 to the point marked "2nd time to Coda ⊕"—then skip to the section marked "Coda.")*

*D. S. 𝄋 al Coda ⊕*

⊕ *Coda*

Lass auch dir die Brust be - we - gen, Lieb - chen, hö - re

mich! be - bend harr' ich dir ent - ge - gen,

komm,_ be - glü - cke

160

mich! Komm, be-glü - cke mich, _____ be-
glü - cke mich!

Don't let the time signature of $\frac{12}{8}$ disturb you. You may think of it made up of two measures of $\frac{6}{8}$. If the range is too high for your voice, put a capo on the third or fourth fret and sing an octave lower than written.

## Che Fiero Costume

Giovanni Legrenzi
(1625-1690)

Fast and spirited

Che fie - ro co - stu - me d'a li - ge - ro nu - me che a
cru - do des - ti - no che un cie - co bam - bi - no con

for - za di pe - ne si fac-cia a - do-rar, si fac-cia a - do-rar, _____ che a
boc - ca di lat - te si fac - cia sti-mar, si fac-cia sti-mar, _____ Con

for - za di pe - ne si fac-cia a - do-rar.
boc - ca di lat - te si fac - cia sti-mar.

E pur nell' ar-do - re il dio tra-di - to-re un
Ma ques-to ti - ran-no con bar-bar-o in-gon-no en-

162

va - go sem - bian - te mi fe'i' do la trar,_____ un va - go sem - bian - te mi
tron - do per gli oc - chi mi fe' do - spi - rar,_____ en - tran - do per gli oc - chi mi

fe'i' do la - trar.  Che fie - ro co - stu - me d'a li - ge - ro nu - me che a
fe so - spi - rar.  Che cru - do des - ti - no che un cie - co bam - bi - no con

for - za di pe - ne si fac - cia a - do - rar, si fac - cia a - do - rar!_____ Che a
boc - ca di lat - te si fac - cia sti - mar, si fac - cia sti - mar!_____ Con

for - za di pe - ne si fac - cia a - do - rar.
boc - ca di lat - te si fac - cia sti - mar.

Che

163

# Plaisir D'Amour

Jean Paul Martini
(1741–1816)

164

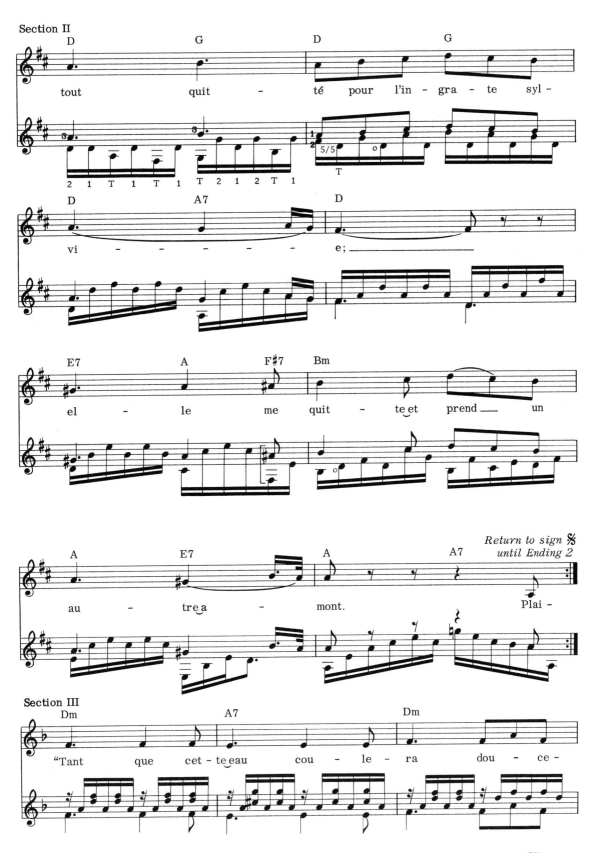

165

ment _____ vers ce ruis - seau qui
bor - de la - prai - ri - e
je t'ai - me - rai,"
Me ré - pé - tait\_\_\_\_ Syl - vi - e.
L'eau cou\_\_\_ le en - core, _____ el -

166

*Return to sign 𝄋*
*until Ending 3*
*(Final Ending)*

le a___ chan - gé___ pour - tant.___ Plai -

# Im Wunderschönen Monat Mai

Words by
Heinrich Heine

Music by
Robert Schumann
(1810–1856)

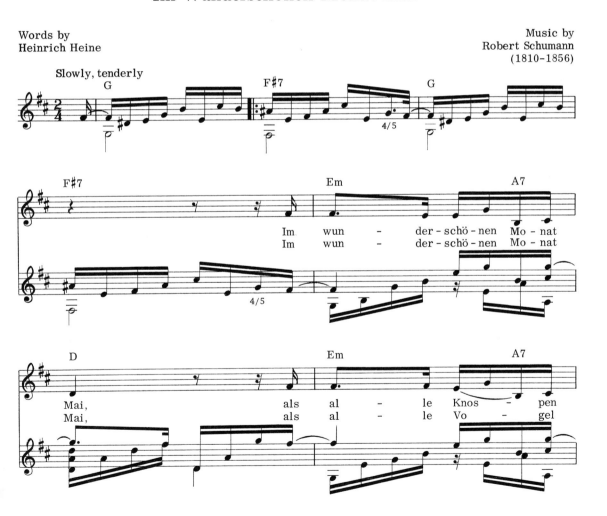

Im wun - der - schö - nen Mo - nat
Im wun - der - schö - nen Mo - nat

Mai,           als al - le Knos - pen
Mai,           als al - le Vo - gel

# Nochi Bezumniye

Words by
Alexei Apukhtin
(1853-1893)
Music: Traditional

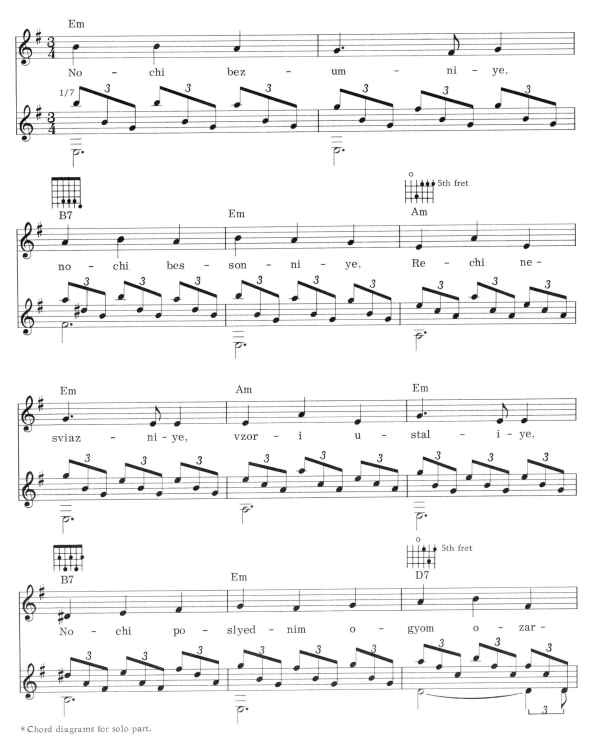

*Chord diagrams for solo part.

169

```
Em                     B7              Em
Pust dazhe vremya rookoi besposhschadnoyoo

Am       Em      Am        Em
Mnye ookazalo chto bylo b Vas lozhnovo,

B7           Em           D7         G
Vsyo zhe lechoo ya k Vam pamiatyoo zhadnoyoo

 Am        Em      B7       C
V proshlom otveta ishchoo nevozmozhnovo.

Am       Em      Am       Em
Nochi bezumniye, nochi bessonniye.
```

```
Em                   B7             Em
Nochi bezumniye, nochi bessonniye,

 Am         Em      Am         Em
V kradchevym shopotom Vy zaglooshayetye

B7           Em      D7        G
Zvooki gynevniye, nesnosniye, shumniye,

 Am        Em          B7       C
B tikhooyoo noch Vy moi son otgoniayetye.

Am       Em      Am      E
Nochi bessonniye, nochi bezumniye.
```

In the second act of Mozart's *Don Giovanni* the Don sings this serenade while languidly "strumming" on a guitar. Meanwhile in the orchestra pit the tinkling notes of a mandolin are heard. The mandolin soloist is anything but languid.

See what you can do with it.

## Deh Vieni Alla Finestra

W. A. Mozart
(1756–1791)

173

# Note Reading

## The Open Strings

The notation of music is done on the lines and in the spaces of a five-lined system called a staff.

These lines and spaces take on specific note names when we add a *G clef*. The G clef gets its name from its shape and from the fact that its lower loop curves around the G line on the staff.

To write notes above or below the staff, we use ledger lines. These lines may be thought of as either higher or lower extensions of the original five lines of the staff.

These notes all may be played on the guitar. Among them are the six open strings.

In playing the following exercises use the thumb for the notes on the sixth, fifth, and fourth strings and the first and second fingers *alternately* for the notes on the third, second, and first strings.

Here is an exercise for the open strings of the guitar.

## Rhythm

Up to now we have been concerned only with identifying the six open strings. Before we go any further with the learning of notes, we must introduce the concept of rhythm and note value. Without actually saying so we have assumed that all the notes played up to now were played at a steady speed and that each one had the same time duration as another. The kind of note value we have used to express this relationship is the *quarter note.*

The direction of the stem (up or down) does not affect the note value. It is done for purely typographical purposes, to avoid having the stems extend either too far above or too far below the staff.

A quarter note, in and of itself, gives us no indication of how rapidly it should be played or how long it should remain sounding. A series of quarter notes only indicates that, relative to each other, the notes are equal in time. Considerations of speed (that is, tempo) are left up to the performer or composer.

In a piece of music notes are usually grouped together in short segments containing the same number of beats. These segments are called *measures*. Measures are separated from each other by *bar lines*.

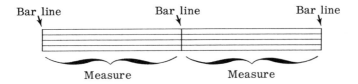

When there are two quarter notes in a measure, the *time signature* will be $\frac{2}{4}$ ("two-four"). This time signature is written at the beginning of the piece and, unless specifically indicated elsewhere, applies to every measure in the piece.

Two-four time, $\frac{2}{4}$, is the most basic metrical arrangement of beats within a musical measure. We walk, run, and breathe in $\frac{2}{4}$.

When playing a piece in $\frac{2}{4}$, start by counting slowly and evenly "one-two one-two one-two . . ." before beginning. Give each "one" a slightly stronger emphasis than "two." Maintain the beat and make sure that the notes you are playing fall on their proper beats.

The following exercises are made up of notes on all the six strings and are written in $\frac{2}{4}$.

## Notes on the E (First) String

**Important:** In the following exercises, when reaching from a note on one fret to a note on a higher fret, do not release the original finger from the lower fret.

This exercise is made up of notes on the first string. Play the notes with the first and second fingers of the right hand alternating.

## Notes on the B (Second) String

176

This exercise is made up of notes on the first and second strings. Continue the alternation of the first and second fingers of the right hand.

## Notes on the G (Third) String

G
Open string

A
Second fret

This exercise is made up of notes on the first three strings. Continue the alternation of the first and second fingers of the right hand.

## Notes on the D (Fourth) String

D
Open string

E
Second fret

F
Third fret

177

This exercise is made up of notes on the first four strings. Use the right thumb to play the notes on the D string and continue the alternation of the first and second fingers on the first three strings as before.

## Notes on the A (Fifth) String

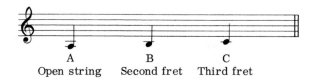

A
Open string

B
Second fret

C
Third fret

This exercise is made up of notes on the first five strings. Use the right thumb to play the notes on the A and D strings and continue the alternation of the first and second fingers on the first three strings as before.

178

# Notes on the E (Sixth) String

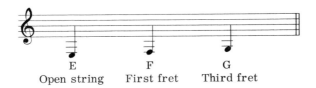

E — Open string    F — First fret    G — Third fret

This exercise is made up of notes on all six strings. Use the right thumb to play the notes on the E, A, and D strings and continue the alternation of the first and second fingers on the first three strings as before.

## Rhythm—Half and Whole Notes

*Four-Quarter* ($\frac{4}{4}$) *Time*

A note whose total time duration is equal to two quarter notes is called a *half note*.

Half note   =   Quarter   +   Quarter

179

A note whose total time duration is equal to four quarter notes is called a *whole note*.

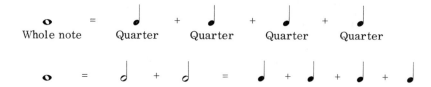

A period of silence is called a *rest*. There is a corresponding rest for every note value.

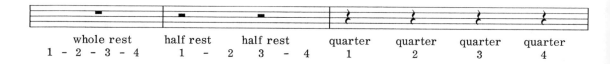

When the measures of a piece of music have four beats, the piece is in four-quarter time, $\frac{4}{4}$. In four-quarter (also called "four-four") time the first and the third beats usually get somewhat heavier accents than the second and fourth.

## We Shall Overcome

*Three-Quarter* $\left(\frac{3}{4}\right)$ *Time*

To write a note whose total time duration is equal to three quarter notes, we must introduce a new musical symbol: the *dot*. A dot coming after a note increases that note's value by one half its original value. Thus,

180

a dotted half note would be equal to a half plus half of a half—that is, a quarter—or, a total time value of three quarters.

If the time duration of a note extends beyond the confines of one measure, we write that note again in the next measure and join the two notes (of the same pitch) with a curved line known as a *tie*. Only the first note of the tied pair is played. The counting is then continued for the total time of the tied notes.

## On Top Of Old Smoky

### The Eighth Note

A note whose time duration is equal to half a quarter note is called an *eighth note*. Eighth notes may be written singly or in groups.

eighth rest

To time the playing of eighth notes properly, we must subdivide the basic "one-two one-two . . ." of the quarter notes into the exactly twice as fast "one-and-two-and one-and-two-and . . ." of the eighth notes.

181

## Black-Eyed Susie

### The Dotted Quarter Note

A dotted quarter note is equal in time to three eighth notes.

It may be found in music in $\frac{2}{4}$, $\frac{4}{4}$, and $\frac{3}{4}$.

## Hold The Fort

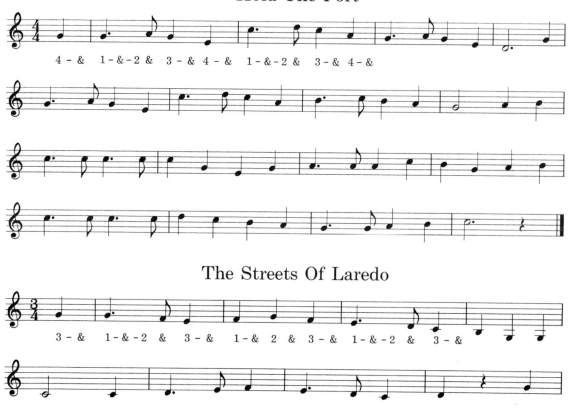

## The Streets Of Laredo

## Six-Eight (6/8) Time

When the unit of beat is the eighth note and there are six eighth notes per measure, the piece is in 6/8. In 6/8 the eighth note gets one count and the quarter note gets two. Usually the accent falls on the first and fourth eighth notes.

### Irish Washerwoman

## The Sixteenth Note

Four sixteenth notes equal one quarter note (or two eighth notes). Sixteenth notes may appear singly, but more often they come in pairs or sets of four.

In order to time the playing of sixteenth notes properly we must subdivide the basic "one-two . . ." of the quarter notes or the twice as fast "one-and-two-and" of the eighth notes into the exactly four times as fast "one-uh-and-uh two-uh-and-uh" of the desired sixteenth notes.

## Soldier's Joy

## Devil's Dream

## The Dotted Eighth and Sixteenth

A dotted eighth is equal to three sixteenths. This note is usually followed by a sixteenth. The whole figure, then, equals one quarter.

In the playing of music containing this figure care must be taken to give it the proper "snap." One must get the feel of the three-times-as-long dotted eighth followed by the very "short" sound of the sixteenth. Counting is as important here as with any other rhythmic figure, but too much of "one-uh-and-uh . . ." will tend to slow the music down beyond the point of recognition.

## Tramp, Tramp, Tramp

185

### The Triplet

If a quarter note is subdivided into three equal parts, we have a *triplet*.

Tying together the first two eighth notes of the triplet, we get the following figure.

Remember that because of the triplet sign this "quarter" and "eighth" combination adds up to one quarter note. We started by subdividing a quarter note—so we still have the original quarter note value under the triplet bracket. This rhythmic figure sounds something like the dotted eighth-sixteenth combination, but there is a difference. Here the first note gets two counts to the second note's one. With the dotted eighth and sixteenth the ratio of first to second note is three to one.

These triplet figures occur very often in blues.

### Jerry's Blues

## Accidentals: Sharps and Flats

The notes comprising the exercises and songs we have played up to now are what are called *natural notes*. They are by no means the only notes available to us. To play these other notes, we need two additional symbols: the *sharp sign* and the *flat sign*.

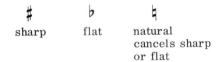

A sharp sign appearing directly in front of a note raises that note by one fret.

A flat sign appearing directly in front of a note lowers that note by one fret.

Up to now we have played everything in a key with no sharps or flats—the key of C. Now we will take a look at some of the keys that folk guitarists play in other than C.

## The Key of G Major

The key of G major has a *key signature* of one sharp—F sharp.

187

This key signature of F sharp applies to each and every note F that may appear in the piece subsequently—high or low. F sharp is played at the following frets.

Here is the G major scale.

## Gee, But I Want To Go Home

## Paper Of Pins

Play the songs in the previous sections of the book which are in the key of G.

# The Key of D Major

The key of D major has a key signature of two sharps—F sharp and C sharp. C sharp is played at the following frets.

Here is the D major scale.

## Blue-Tail Fly

## On Springfield Mountain

Play the songs in the previous sections of the book which are in the key of D.

## The Key of A Major

The key of A major has a key signature of three sharps—F sharp, C sharp, and G sharp. G sharp is played at the following frets.

Here is the A-major scale.

## The Sow Took The Measles

## Villikins And His Dinah

Play the songs in the previous sections of the book which are in the key of A.

## The Key of E Major

The key of E major has a key signature of four sharps—F sharp, C sharp, G sharp, and D sharp. D sharp is played at the following frets.

D sharps

4/1    2/4

Here is the E-major scale.

A-Roving

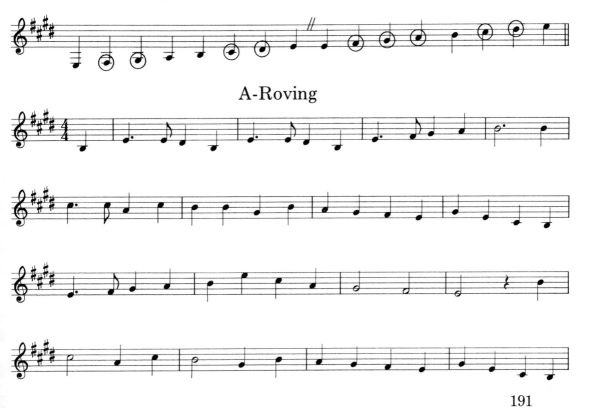

191

## Barbara Allen

Play the songs in the previous sections of the book which are in the key of E.

This completes the basic five keys (C,G,D,A,E) generally encountered in folk guitar arrangements. In addition there is one other major key which is occasionally used.

## The Key of F Major

The key of F major has a key signature of one flat—B flat. B flat is played at the following frets.

Here is the F-major scale.

## The Grey Goose

# The Foggy, Foggy Dew

Before considering the remaining keys it will be useful to study the following *chromatic scales* containing all the sharps and all the flats fret by fret.

## The Chromatic Scale with Sharps

# The Chromatic Scale with Flats

## The Remaining Sharp Keys

B major

F# major

C# major

## The Remaining Flat Keys

Bb major

E♭ major

A♭ major

D♭ major

G♭ major

C♭ major

# The Theory of Chord Construction

An understanding of how chords are constructed is of paramount importance to guitarists. Chords are combinations of notes grouped according to certain principles. Those principles are expressed in terms of *intervals*.

## Intervals

A musical interval is the distance between two notes. We measure this distance in units known as *half steps* (or *minor seconds*). A half step is played on the guitar by moving from one fret to its immediate upper or lower neighbor.

When an open string is involved, a half step up is the first fret and a half step down is the fourth fret of the next lower string. (A half step below the B string is the third fret of the G string.)

# Combining Intervals to Form Chords

## Major Chords

A major chord is constructed of three notes that have the following interval relationship:

note—*4 half steps*—note—*3 half steps*—note

Another term for four half steps is a *major third.*
Another term for three half steps is a *minor third.*
Our definition of a major chord may, therefore, be altered to:

note—*major third*—note—*minor third*—note

If you check back to the major scales in Section Seven, you will note that major chords may also be considered to be built upon the *first, third,* and *fifth* notes of their corresponding scales.

*Minor Chords*

A minor chord is constructed of three notes that have the following interval relationship:

note—*3 half steps*—note—*4 half steps*—note
(*minor 3rd*)　　　　(*major 3rd*)

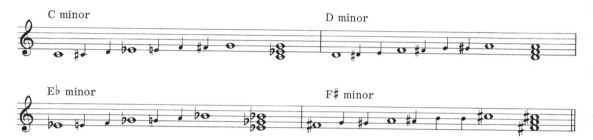

*Dominant-Seventh Chords*

A dominant-seventh chord (usually referred to by guitarists as a "seventh chord," *e.g.,* G7, D7, etc.) is constructed of four notes that have the following interval relationship:

note—*4 half steps*—note—*3 half steps*—note—*3 half steps*—note.
(*major 3rd*)　　　　(*minor 3rd*)　　　　(*minor 3rd*)

As you can see, a dominant-seventh chord is a major chord to which is added a higher minor third.

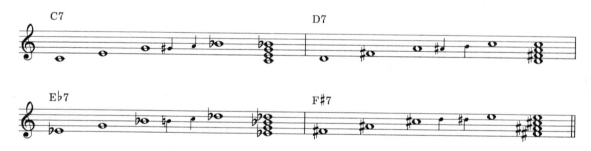

*Minor-Seventh Chords*

A minor-seventh chord (usually written as Gm7, Dm7, etc.) is constructed of four notes that have the following interval relationship:

note—*3 half steps*—note—*4 half steps*—note—*3 half steps*—note
(*minor 3rd*)　　　　(*major 3rd*)　　　　(*minor 3rd*)

As you can see, a minor-seventh chord is a minor chord to which is added a higher minor third.

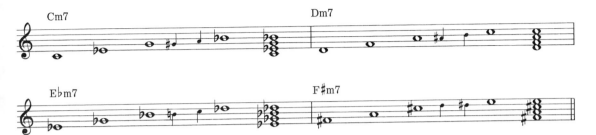

## Diminished-Seventh Chords

A diminished-seventh chord (usually referred to by guitarists as a "diminished chord," *e.g.*, Gdim, Ddim) is constructed of four notes that have the following interval relationship:

note—*3 half steps*—note—*3 half steps*—note—*3 half steps*—note
  (*minor 3rd*)  (*minor 3rd*)  (*minor 3rd*)

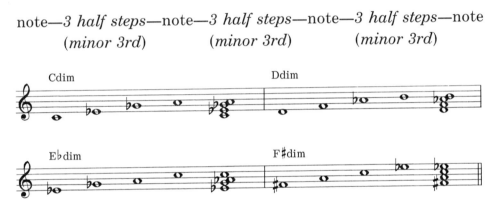

## Major-Seventh Chords

A major-seventh chord (Gmaj7, Dmaj7) is constructed of four notes that have the following interval relationship:

note—*4 half steps*—note—*3 half steps*—note—*4 half steps*—note
  (*major 3rd*)  (*minor 3rd*)  (*major 3rd*)

As you can see, a major-seventh chord is a major chord to which is added a higher major third.

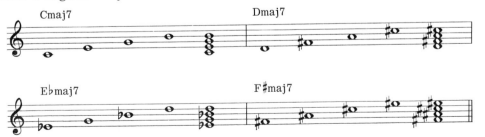

*Minor-Sixth Chords*

A minor sixth chord (Gm6, Dm6) is constructed of four notes with the following interval relationship:

note—*3 half steps*—note—*4 half steps*—note—*2 half steps*—note
     (*minor 3rd*)          (*major 3rd*)          (*major 2nd*)

As you can see, a minor-sixth chord is a minor chord to which is added a higher major second (two half steps).

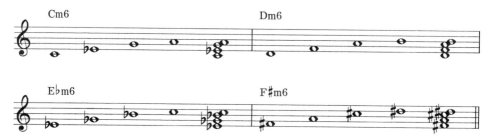

*Augmented Chords*

An augmented chord (Gaug or G+, Daug or D+) is constructed of three notes that have the following interval relationship:

note—*4 half steps*—note—*4 half steps*—note
     (*major 3rd*)          (*major 3rd*)

As you can see, an augmented chord resembles a major chord whose highest note (the *fifth*—remember 1-3-5) has been raised a half step.

*Suspended Chords*

A suspension is a note present in a chord which, strictly speaking, does not belong there. In traditional harmony it is there because it has been "left over"—literally "suspended"—from the preceding chord. Customarily the suspended note is the fourth note of the scale. When present it takes the place of the third note.

Common suspended chords are alterations of major and dominant-seventh chords. They are referred to by guitarists variously as "sus 4" (Gsus4, Dsus4) and have the following interval relationship:

note—*5 half steps*—note—*2 half steps*—note
(*perfect 4th*)     (*major 2nd*)

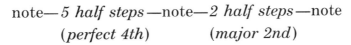

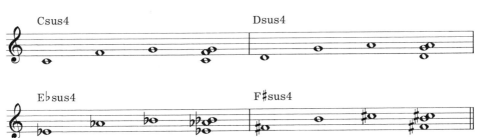

or as "7sus4" (G7sus4, D7sus4)—with the following interval relationship:

note—*5 half steps*—note—*2 half steps*—note—*3 half steps*—note
(*perfect 4th*)     (*major 2nd*)     (*minor 3rd*)

# Tuning the Guitar

Tuning any instrument is a process of trial and error. It involves comparing a standard pitch with the note you are trying to tune and making the necessary adjustments in that note. The degree of accuracy in tuning depends upon your ability to hear small differences in pitch. This ability is present in varying degrees of refinement in different people. It can be sharpened, to some extent, by exposure to the tuning process itself and by "knowing what to listen for."

The pitch of a string—on a guitar, for example—is dependent upon three factors, two of which are variable and one of which is relatively fixed. The variables are the length and the tension of the string, the fixed factor is the string's diameter.

If you shorten the vibrating length of a string by pressing down at some fret, the pitch will rise proportionately. If you lengthen the same string by pressing down at a lower fret or playing the string open again, the pitch will fall.

If you tighten a string by turning the tuning peg, the pitch will rise. Loosening the string, by turning the peg in the opposite direction, lowers the pitch.

As far as changing the diameter is concerned, this can be done, obviously, only by playing another string. The smaller the diameter the higher the pitch—the greater the diameter the lower the pitch.

There are a number of practical ways to tune the guitar.

The guitar may be tuned to a piano. If this is done you must be aware of the fact that the strings of the guitar sound an octave lower than they are usually written. The relationship between guitar strings and piano keys is the following:

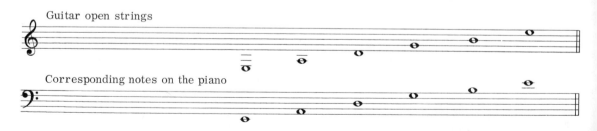

202

Remember, though, that even if you play the same notes on the piano as on the guitar *a piano will not sound like a guitar*. This difference in tonal quality (*timbre*) may be confusing at first, but it can be overcome. A good way to bridge the gap between the two instruments is to sing or hum the desired note and tune the guitar to your voice. While there is a difference between the timbres of piano, voice, and guitar, once we really hear the pitch "inside" ourselves we have taken a great step forward in the tuning process.

A *guitar pitch pipe* will give the actual pitch of the six strings.

If no standard pitch is available, the guitar may be tuned *relative to itself*. This is the most basic way of tuning the instrument, and it requires the most careful listening. It can be attempted only after you have had some experience playing and have some idea of what an "in tune" instrument sounds like.

The best way to begin tuning using this process (or indeed any other method) is first to determine if your instrument is out of tune. If you cannot tell by playing the open strings then play an E minor chord slowly—string by string. Listen closely for any note that may seem out of order. If a string seems off, you must decide whether it is too high or too low and then tighten or loosen it according to your determination.

If the sixth (E) string seems to be all right, you can make the following check on the others:

The *fifth fret* of the sixth string is A. This should sound the same as the fifth string.

The *fifth fret* of the fifth string is D. This should sound the same as the fourth string.

The *fifth fret* of the fourth string is G. This should sound the same as the third string.

The *fourth fret* of the third string is B. This should sound the same as the second string.

The *fifth fret* of the second string is E. This should sound the same as the first string.

The first string (E) should then be compared with the sixth string (E—two octaves lower).

Play a few chords string by string and listen closely—you may have to repeat this tuning process a number of times before you are completely satisfied.

Another relative pitch method involves tuning the open strings to each other. This is done by "hearing" the musical interval between adjacent strings. E-A, A-D, D-G, B-E are *perfect fourths*. G-B is a *major third*.

A perfect fourth may be sung easily if you think of the first two notes of *When Johnny Comes Marching Home, Home on the Range, Aura Lee, Funiculi, Funicula, Froggie Went A-Courting, Taps,* and many other songs.

A major third may be sung easily if you think of the first two notes of *Michael, Row the Boat Ashore, Kum Ba Ya, When I First Came to This Land,* and many others. You can even play part of *Taps* on the D, G, and B strings to check on their tuning.

---

### Basic Guitar Chords (See pages 206–207)

Key to symbols employed in this chart:

P = Primary Bass String
A = Alternate Bass String
x = String Not to Be Played
o = Open String to Be Played
③ = Finger May Be Moved for Alternate Bass
⌒ = Barre

*Note:* The numbers immediately to the right of some of the diagrams indicate the fret at which the chord is to begin.

# Transposing

A piece of music or a song may be played and sung in any key. In the learning of chords and instrumental technique you may have found that some of the songs that illustrated the material were either too high or too low for you. The keys of these songs may be changed (*transposed*) to more comfortable ones depending upon your voice.

Most simple folk songs can be harmonized by using three chords. For example: C, F, G7 or D, G, A7. If you check back at the scales you will see that these chords are based on the first, fourth, and fifth notes of their respective keys. These I, IV, and V chords are the backbone of our musical system. Any song starting with C could just as well start with D, G, or any other note providing the relationships among the following chords are maintained.

*Table of I, IV, and V₍₇₎ Chords*

| KEY | I | IV | V$_{(7)}$ |
|---|---|---|---|
| C | C | F | G |
| G | G | C | D |
| D | D | G | A |
| A | A | D | E |
| E | E | A | B |
| B | B | E | F♯ |
| F♯ (G♭) | F♯ (G♭) | B (C♭) | C♯ (D♭) |
| C♯ (D♭) | C♯ (D♭) | F♯ (G♭) | G♯ (A♭) |
| A♭ | A♭ | D♭ | E♭ |
| E♭ | E♭ | A♭ | B♭ |
| B♭ | B♭ | E♭ | F |
| F | F | B♭ | C |

The I chord is called the *tonic;* the IV, the *subdominant;* the V, the *dominant.*

As you know, these three chords are not the only chords found in many songs. The number of possibilities is virtually unlimited—depending upon the style and period of the music. The process of transposition, however, remains the same: Determine the relationships between the chords in the

205

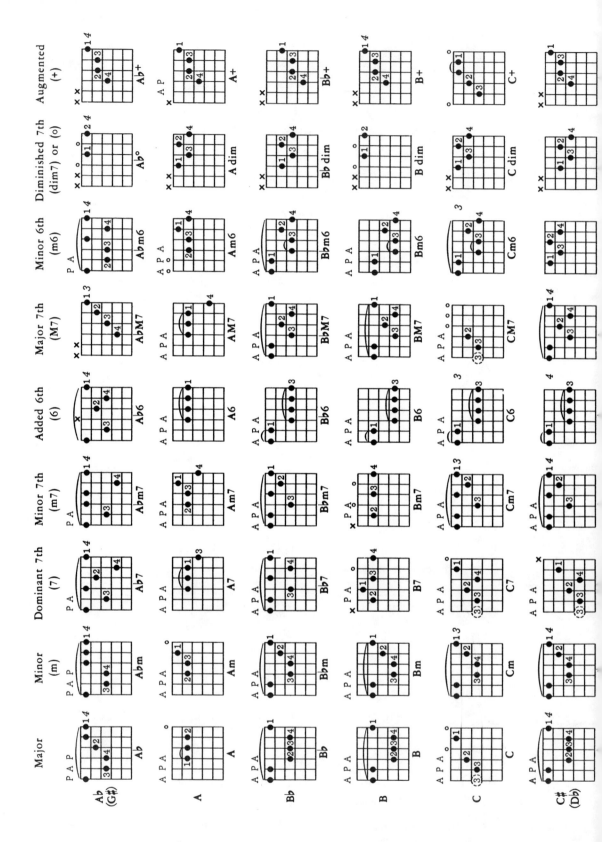

206

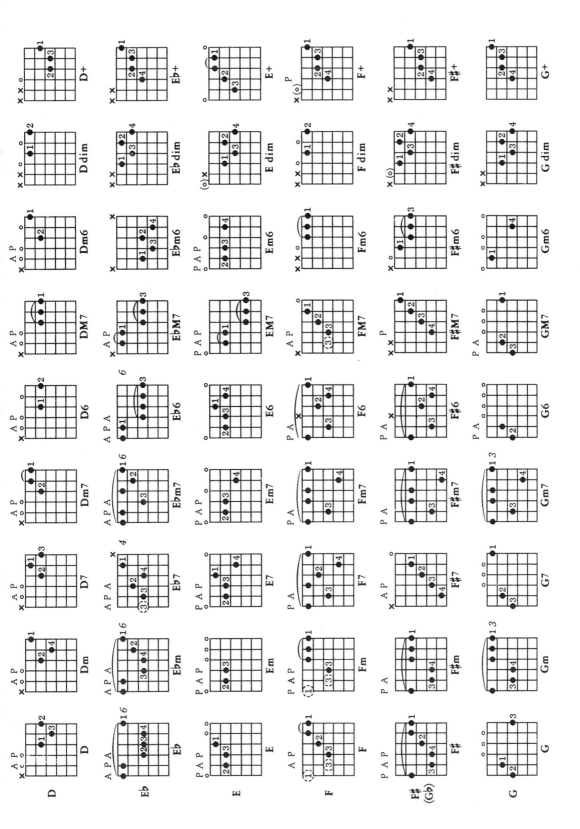

207

original key and then substitute chords with the same relationships in the new key.

*Remember the key signatures* when transposing. C major is the only major key without sharps or flats—and the chords in C reflect this.

All other keys will have at least one chord with a sharp or flat in its spelling. The following table will illustrate chords for the six common folk guitar keys.

*Key*                                                       *Chords*

| Key | I | II | III | IV | V | VI | VIII |
|-----|-----|-----|------|-----|-----|------|-------|
| C | C | Dm | Em | F | G | Am | Bdim |
| G | G | Am | Bm | C | D | Em | F♯dim |
| D | D | Em | F♯m | G | A | Bm | C♯dim |
| A | A | Bm | C♯m | D | E | F♯m | G♯dim |
| E | E | F♯m | G♯m | A | B | C♯m | D♯dim |
| F | F | Gm | Am | B♭ | C | Dm | Edim |

## The Capo

For playing characteristic, graceful folk style accompaniments in all keys a *capo* is highly recommended. The capo is an elastic or metal clamp that fits over all the strings at a particular fret and raises the pitch of the guitar by that many frets (half steps). In effect, it transposes the guitar.

If a song in the key of G, say, is too low for you—try putting the capo on the third fret. This will give you the key of B flat. You should refer to the chromatic scales on page 193–194 to see what new chords are arrived at by moving familiar chords up by means of a capo. (C up one fret is C sharp, up three frets is E flat—and so on.)